TEACHER'S BOOK OF

PLAYS

AND CHORAL READINGS

Printed on recycled paper.

Macmillan/McGraw-Hill School Publishing Company
New York ▪ Chicago ▪ Columbus

READERS THEATER PLAYS

CONT

ENTS

CORRELATIONS

Each play and choral reading selection has been developed to reinforce the unit theme in the Student Anthology

UNIT THEMES, PLAYS, AND CHORAL READINGS

Unit 3   Teaming Up

Theme: People and animals working together
Play: *A Whale of a Story* — a video newscast about people's efforts to free a whale trapped behind the the Liberty Island Bridge in the Sacramento River in 1981
Choral Reading: *The Erie Canal* — a classic American folk song about the partnership of a mule driver and his mule Sal

Level 7
Unit 1   You've Got the Write Idea!

Theme: Writing to communicate ideas and feelings and to get things done
Play: *Mother Goose to the Rescue* — a nursery-rhyme spoof that centers around the advice column of the *Mother Goose Gazette*
Choral Reading: *My Autograph Album* — a series of autograph rhymes

Unit 2   Better Together

Theme: Working things out and cooperating with friends
Play: *I'll Be the Dragon!* — a realistic play-within-a-play that focuses on learning to cooperate with classmates while rehearsing a Readers Theater presentation
Choral Reading: *Helping* and *Changing* — poems about cooperation and friendship

Unit 3   Water, Water Everywhere

Theme: The power and properties of water
Play: *The Search for the Magic Lake* — a dramatization of an Ecuadorian folk tale that describes a young girl's heroic search for the curative water of a magic lake
Choral Reading: *One Misty, Moisty Morning* and *Sound of Water* — poems about water

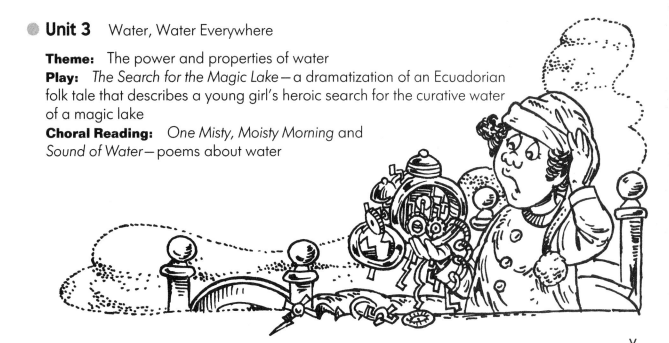

INTRODUCTION

Weread for many different reasons, but chief among them should be the discovery that reading can be both fun and purposeful. And what could be more entertaining than working together to make words come alive in a Readers Theater or choral reading presentation? This book of plays and choral readings has been developed to give you and your students an opportunity to enjoy reading aloud together. At the same time, your students will be developing their reading fluency skills through these enjoyable and motivating oral-reading experiences.

The following pages provide a compilation of hints and tips gathered from teachers who have made oral-reading techniques work in their classrooms. Unlike dramatic productions requiring memorization, elaborate sets, costumes, and stage directions, Readers Theater and choral reading only require a set of scripts and a group of enthusiastic readers—the former you are holding, while the latter wait in the wings of your classroom!

READERS THEATER—A DESCRIPTION

Readers Theater has been used by teachers for many years. Also known as Dramatic Reading, Chamber Theater, or Story Theater, the name Readers Theater seems most appropriate because it puts the emphasis where it belongs—on the *reading* rather than the memorization of a script. Unlike traditional drama, in which performers memorize lines and move about a stage, Readers Theater is simply the rehearsed oral reading of a script by a group of performers. It requires no training in drama or the performing arts on the part of students or teachers; there are no complicated guidelines to follow. While simple costumes or backdrops can be used to help establish characterization and setting, they are optional. The fact that Readers Theater involves such simple techniques makes it a viable option for every classroom.

READERS THEATER AND CHORAL READING—THE BENEFITS

Among the chief benefits of Readers Theater and choral reading is the development of oral-reading fluency. Identified by some reading authorities as a frequently "neglected goal" of reading instruction, fluency training has been recognized as an important aspect of proficient reading.

Two essential components for successful fluency training are repeated reading and active listening. Most students can sharpen their active listening skills by attending while the teacher reads aloud for a brief period every day. However, convincing students to repeatedly read the same selection orally until fluency is achieved is quite a different matter. Usually the response is less than enthusiastic.

Enter Readers Theater and choral reading!—both natural partners for fluency training. The oral reading of plays and poetry generates a natural excitement and a willingness to rehearse that enables teachers to integrate repeated reading practice into their instructional program. The goal of a polished performance is a genuinely motivating force that provides a rationale for the fluency training that all students need.

Readers Theater and choral reading offer students a *meaningful* context in which to practice expression, shading, phrasing, diction, pitch, and rate, as well as word recognition skills. (For additional information on fluency training and its benefits, see the articles listed in the Bibliography.)

Readers Theater and choral reading also develop active listening skills on the part of both participants and audience. Readers must listen attentively to pick up on cues or to chime in as a member of a group. Audience members also are encouraged to sharpen listening skills as they interpret the dialog and narration to visualize settings and characters that are described rather than visibly presented on stage.

In addition to developing fluency skills, Readers Theater and choral reading can also help students internalize literature, thereby improving their comprehension. Dramatizations enable readers to "become" the characters they play. What better way to reinforce character and plot development than through plays? Dramatizations also expose students to the rich heritage of oral language and storytelling. Through the oral reading of scripts and poetry, students internalize the rhythm of repeated refrains, certain language conventions, and traditional story structure.

A final benefit of Readers Theater and choral reading is derived from the high levels of student interaction and involvement within cooperative learning groups. Through these shared oral-reading experiences, students learn to work together, take turns, listen to each other, and employ group decision-making and problem-solving strategies in casting and production decisions.

Unlike many group activities in which all participants must function on or about the same level to effectively complete the task, a Readers Theater group using the scripts in this book can be composed of students with widely differing reading abilities. The scripts have been written to include roles of varying length and difficulty, enabling students of all ability levels to fully participate and contribute to the achievement of the common goal: a shared oral-reading experience.

LAUNCHING READERS THEATER IN YOUR CLASSROOM

As the following steps indicate, introducing Readers Theater to your class is a straightforward procedure. The only rules are: Keep it simple! and Keep it fun!

1. SCRIPT PREPARATION

Decide when you want to introduce the Readers Theater play within a unit. Then duplicate a copy of the script for each cast member and the director. (Since scripts sometimes have a habit of disappearing, you might make a few extras, just in case.) Students can make construction-paper covers, using the full-page art that precedes each script for decoration, if they wish.

2. ROLE ASSIGNMENT

The plays in this collection were purposefully written with roles requiring varying levels of reading proficiency. Initially you may want to take into account individual reading ability when making role assignments, but once students have become familiar with a play, roles can and should be switched. Because the characters are read rather than acted, the part of a boy can be read by a girl and vice versa. As students become familiar with Readers Theater, they should be encouraged to assume responsibility for casting decisions as they participate within the cooperative decision-making environment of a Readers Theater group.

3. REHEARSALS

In the first rehearsal, students in the cast should sit together in a Readers Theater group—perhaps gathered around a table—and read through the script to get a sense of the plot and characters. If the play is an adaptation, you may want to read aloud the original story. (Sources for stories that have been adapted appear in the Bibliography.) At this time, roles should be assigned or agreed upon, and students can be encouraged to identify their lines with a transparent highlighter.

Subsequent rehearsals should include paired repeated readings where two characters rehearse their lines together. Having a tape recorder available for these readings will enable students to evaluate their progress. In these early rehearsals, students should focus on word recognition and on listening for cues. Once these goals have been achieved, attention can be turned to articulation, expression, rate, shading, and phrasing. Invite students to make "reader's notes" in pencil in their scripts. A slash, for example, can be used as a reminder of a pause not indicated by punctuation. An underline can indicate that a word needs special emphasis. These notations can be a valuable aid to oral reading.

During rehearsals, students may decide to add their own personal touches to a script. If the cast decides to add, delete, or alter a speech, this change should be made in all copies of the script.

4. BLOCKING AND FOCUS

In Readers Theater, the performers usually do not move about the stage. However, there are two bits of "stage business" that require rehearsal—where the performers will sit in relation to each other, and where they should look when they are speaking.

Each play is accompanied by a blocking diagram that suggests a seating arrangement. Before the performance, students will need to practice entering, assuming their places on stools or chairs, and exiting. If music stands are available, you may wish to have students use them to hold their scripts during a performance. In some cases, a music stand for the narrator has been suggested in the blocking diagram.

Focus should be an important part of the rehearsal process because, with the exception of a simple gesture or two, focus is the only direct action employed during a Readers Theater presentation. Basically, there are two kinds of focus that students can use: on-stage and off-stage focus. In on-stage focus, the characters look at each other when they speak. In off-stage focus, the characters direct their gaze to a spot on the wall behind the audience. In both types of focus, it is important that students be familiar enough with their lines so their eyes and heads are up rather than buried in a script.

5. PROPS AND COSTUMES

While elaborate costumes and props are not necessary for Readers Theater, even the simplest costumes, such as hats, scarves, or animal ears can help students assume their character. Costume suggestions can be found on the resource pages following several of the plays.

Making background murals or very simple props can help students deepen their understanding of a play. Involvement in discussions about what to emphasize in a drawing or in the scenery or about which free-standing props would suggest the setting (a tree) or occasion (a birthday cake) allows a further involvement and commitment on the part of participants. Either the performers or another group of students acting as stage crew can create the props and costumes.

Hand-held props are not suggested for Readers Theater because the hands should be free to hold the script. For a similar reason, masks should be avoided since they may impair the performers' ability to see the script or project the lines.

6. THE STAGE

Readers Theater does not require a proscenium stage with a curtain, just an open area with enough space for the cast and an audience. A corner of the classroom will work as well as the school auditorium. For plays that lend themselves to puppet dramatizations, simple directions for both the puppets and the stage are included in the resource pages. In staging a Readers Theater puppet show, it generally works best to have one cast read the script while another cast operates the puppets.

7. SHARING THE PERFORMANCE

Readers Theater presentations are meant to be shared, but the audience can range from one person to a packed auditorium. Before the performance begins, you or a student may wish to briefly introduce the conventions of Readers Theater so that the audience understands its role in interpreting dialog to visualize the characters and the action. Students may enjoy making programs, tickets, and posters for the production, especially if another class or parents are invited to attend. On the day of the performance, have the characters enter, take their places, and read!

8. PERFORMANCE FOLLOW-UP

After the performance, suggest that the cast gather to discuss their reading of the play. To guide their discussion, they may use the Self-Evaluation Form. By assessing their own performances as readers, as listeners, and as group members, students can set personal goals to work toward during their next oral-reading experience.

THE CHORAL READING EXPERIENCE

Choral reading, like Readers Theater, is an activity that promotes fluency through cooperative effort. In choral reading, speaking and listening are complementary processes—groups of students practice reading poetry for another group to listen to. During practice sessions, the group will need a director, usually the teacher in the early sessions. As students become more experienced with this technique, they can explore taking on the responsibilities of the director.

TYPES OF CHORAL READING

Choral reading promotes fluency by giving support to readers, by providing an opportunity for repeated reading with special attention to rhythm and meter, and by encouraging active listening. The four major types of choral reading are

- refrain
- antiphonal
- line-by-line
- unison

In a poem with a refrain, the verse can be read by a solo voice, by a group (the most common choice), or in combination. In line-by-line choral reading, each line or group of lines is read by a different group or solo voice. Antiphonal choral readings are somewhat like call and response, with one group answering another. Unison readings—perhaps the most difficult of all—are read by the entire group.

The choral readings for each unit have suggestions for groups and solo voices. Your students should first try reading the poems as arranged. After they are familiar with a particular reading, encourage them to try other arrangements or other poems.

SIZE AND ORGANIZATION OF THE CHORAL READING GROUP

You and your students may want to experiment with the size of the choral reading group, which will vary depending upon the number of students who want to participate and the particular piece being performed. Most often, members of a group should stand together. Sometimes, readers with solo parts are also part of a group. In these cases, the soloists should stand in the front row of the group. Resource pages suggest arrangements of speakers for choral reading.

THE RESOURCE PAGES

This book includes both teacher and student resource pages. Resource pages follow the plays and always include a blocking diagram for the play. Other resource pages may include costume suggestions and patterns, a pronunciation guide, prop suggestions, puppets, puppet-show directions, sound effects, and audiotaping instructions for radio plays. Resource pages for the choral readings include blocking diagrams. The final resource page is a self-evaluation form for readers and listeners.

BIBLIOGRAPHY

ARTICLES ON READING FLUENCY

ALLINGTON, R.L. 1983. Fluency: The neglected reading goal. *The Reading Teacher* 36:556–61.

BEAVER, J.M. 1982. Say it! Over and over. *Language Arts* 59:143–48.

DOWHOWER, S.L. 1987. Effects of repeated reading on second-grade transitional readers' fluency and comprehension. *Reading Research Quarterly* 22:389–406.

—. 1989. Repeated reading: Research into practice. *The Reading Teacher* 42:502–7.

KOSKINEN, P.S., and I.H. BLUM. 1986. Paired repeated reading: A classroom strategy for developing fluent reading. *The Reading Teacher* 40:70–75.

MICCINATI, J.L. 1985. Using prosodic cues to teach oral reading fluency. *The Reading Teacher* 39:206–12.

RASINSKI, T. 1989. Fluency for everyone: Incorporating fluency instruction in the classroom. *The Reading Teacher* 42:690–93.

—, and J.B. ZUTELL. 1990. Making a place for fluency instruction in the regular reading curriculum. *Reading Research and Instruction* 29:85–91.

SAMUELS, S.J. 1988. Decoding and automaticity: Helping poor readers become automatic at word recognition. *The Reading Teacher* 41:756–60.

ARTICLES ON READERS THEATER AND DRAMATIC READING

ANDERSEN, D.R. 1987. Around the world in eighty days. *Instructor* 97(October): 62–63.

—. 1989. The shy exclamation point. *Instructor* 98(February): 54.

—. 1988. The sound of great voices. *Instructor* 97(January): 46–47.

BENNETT, S., and K. BEATTY. 1988. Grades 1 and 2 love readers theatre. *The Reading Teacher* 41:485.

BIDWELL, S.M. 1990. Using drama to increase motivation, comprehension and fluency. *Journal of Reading* 34:38–41.

BURNS, G., and E. KIZER. 1987. Audio-visual effects in readers' theatre: A case study. *International Journal of Instructional Media.* 14(3): 223–37.

DICKINSON, E. 1987. Readers Theatre: A creative method to increase reading fluency and comprehension skills. *The New England Reading Association Journal* 23(22): 7–11.

EPPERHEIMER, D. 1991. Readers' Theatre and technology: A perfect mix. *The California Reader* 24(Spring): 14–15.

FREEDMAN, M. 1990. Readers Theatre: An exciting way to motivate reluctant readers. *The New England Reading Association Journal* 26(Autumn): 9–12.

HOWARD, W.L., and others. 1989. Using choral responding to increase active student response. *Teaching Exceptional Children.* 21(Spring): 72–75.

NAVASCUES, M. 1988. Oral and dramatic interpretation of literature in the Spanish class. *Hispania* 71(March): 186–89.

STEWIG, J.W. 1990. Children's books for readers' theatre. *Perspectives* Spring:vii–x.

BOOKS ON READERS THEATER

BAUER, CAROLINE FELLER. *Celebrations: Read-Aloud Holiday and Theme Book Programs.* New York: H.W. Wilson, 1985.

—. *Presenting Reader's Theatre: Plays and Poems to Read Aloud.* New York: H.W. Wilson, 1987.

COGER, LESLIE IRENE, and MELVIN R. WHITE. *Readers Theatre Handbook: A Dramatic Approach to Literature.* 3d ed. Glenview, Ill.: Scott, Foresman, 1982.

FORKERT, OTTO MAURICE. *Children's Theatre that Captures Its Audience.* Chicago: Coach House Press, 1962.

LAUGHLIN, MILDRED KNIGHT, and KATHY HOWARD LATROBE. *Readers Theatre for Children.* Englewood, Colo.: Teacher Ideas Press, 1990.

SIERRA, JUDY, and ROBERT KAMINSKI. *Twice Upon a Time: Stories to Tell, Retell, Act Out, and Write About.* New York: H.W. Wilson, 1989.

SLOYER, SHIRLEE. *Readers Theatre: Story Dramatization in the Classroom.* Urbana, Ill.: National Council of Teachers of English, 1982.

—. "Readers Theatre: A Reading Motivator." In *Selected Articles on the Teaching of Reading.* New York: Barnell Loft, 1977.

BOOKS ON CHORAL READING

AGGERTT, OTIS J., and ELBERT R. BOWEN. *Communicative Reading.* New York: Macmillan, 1972.

GOTTLIEB, MARVIN R. *Oral Interpretation.* New York: McGraw-Hill, 1980.

JOHNSON, ALBERT, and BERTHA JOHNSON. *Oral Reading: Creative and Interpretive.* South Brunswick: A. S. Barnes, 1971.

BOOKS ON COSTUMES, MAKE-UP, and PROPS

ARNOLD, A. *Arts and Crafts for Children and Young People.* London: Macmillan, 1976.

BARWELL, EVE. *Disguises You Can Make.* New York: Lothrop, Lee & Shepard, 1977.

CHERNOFF, GOLDIE TAUB. *Easy Costumes You Don't Have to Sew.* New York: Four Winds Press, 1975.

HALEY, GAIL E. *Costumes for Plays and Playing.* New York: Metheun, 1982.

Make and Play Paperback Set (includes costumes, face painting, hats, masks, and T-shirt painting). New York: Franklin Watts, 1990.

McCASLIN, NELLIE. *Shows on a Shoestring: An Easy Guide to Amateur Productions.* New York: David McKay, 1979.

MORIN, ALICE. *Newspaper Theatre: Creative Play Production for Low Budgets and No Budgets.* Belmont, Calif.: Fearon Teacher Aids, 1989.

PARISH, PEGGY. *Costumes to Make.* New York: Macmillan, 1970.

PITCHER, CAROLINE, consultant. *Masks and Puppets.* New York: Franklin Watts, 1984.

PURDY, SUSAN. *Costumes for You to Make.* Philadelphia: J.B. Lippincott, 1971.

SOURCES FOR ADAPTATIONS

"Why There Are No Tigers in Borneo." From *Indonesian Legends and Folk Tales* by Adele de Leeuw. New York: Nelson, 1961.

"The Search for the Magic Lake" from *Latin American Tales* by Genevieve Barlow. Chicago: Rand McNally, 1966.

Macmillan/McGraw-Hill

ROOM FOR MORE

ANNE M. MIRANDA

CAST:

NARRATOR	UNCLE LEE
MOM	BUSTER
GRAMPS PIERRE	BILL
GRANDMA CLAIRE	BLAIR
DAD	BOBBIE DEE
MOLLY	PUDDIN'HEAD
AUNTIE JANE	COUSIN SUE

Macmillan/McGraw-Hill

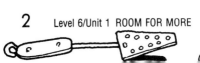

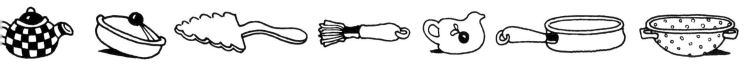

NARRATOR: Once, not very long ago,
Dad fixed a lunch from Mexico:
refried beans and hot tamales—
a favorite dish of daughter Molly's.
Mother made some mango punch.
Then the three sat down to lunch.
Mom was just about to pour,
When someone knocked on the front door.

[Knock, knock!]

MOM: Who's there?

GRAMPS PIERRE: It's Gramps Pierre and Grandma Claire.
We've just come from the county fair.

GRANDMA CLAIRE: We have our little cat, Ling Shoo,
and a pot of Irish stew.

MOM: Molly, would you show them in?

DAD: Sit down and tell us how you've been.

MOLLY: It's good to see you, Grandma Claire.
It's good to see you, Gramps Pierre.

DAD: Come in, come in, and take a chair.

NARRATOR: Gramps sat here and Grandma there.
Ling Shoo curled up beneath a chair.
Mom got each a cup and plate.
Then someone slammed the garden gate.

[Knock, knock!]

MOM: Who can it be?

AUNTIE JANE: It's Auntie Jane and Uncle Lee.
We drove from Knoxville, Tennessee.

UNCLE LEE: So glad you're home. We took a chance.
Here's some cheese from Paris, France.

MOM: Molly, would you show them in?

DAD: Sit down and tell us how you've been.

MOLLY: It's good to see you, Uncle Lee
and Auntie Jane from Tennessee.

Macmillan/McGraw-Hill

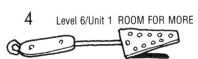

GRAMPS PIERRE: Howdy do!

GRANDMA CLAIRE: How are you?

ALL: Come in, come in!
Sit down! What's new?

NARRATOR: Then Uncle Lee gave Mom the cheese,
while Auntie Jane gave Dad a squeeze.
Just then a car pulled in the drive.
They heard more unexpected guests arrive.

[Knock, knock!]

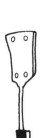
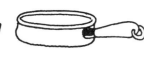

MOM: Who's there?

BUSTER: Your cousins, Buster, Bill, and Blair.

BILL: And Bart, our dog with shaggy hair.

BLAIR: Our mother said it would be nice
to bring a dish of Spanish rice.

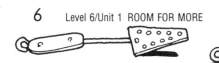

MOM: Molly, would you show them in?

DAD: Sit down and tell us how you've been.

MOLLY: It's good to see you, Bill and Blair,
and Buster and Bart with shaggy hair.

GRAMPS PIERRE: Howdy do!

GRANDMA CLAIRE: How are you?

AUNTIE JANE: Hello there.

UNCLE LEE: Pull up a chair.

ALL: Come in, come in!
There's lots to share!

NARRATOR: The triplets, Buster, Blair, and Bill,
sat upon the windowsill.
And Bart, the dog with shaggy hair,
flopped in Daddy's favorite chair.
There was hardly room for more,
when someone else knocked on the door!

[Knock, knock!]

MOM: Who can it be?

BOBBIE DEE: It's your nephew, Bobbie Dee.
My ship is in. I'm home from sea.

PUDDIN'HEAD: And I'm his parrot, Puddin'head.
We've brought some nice Italian bread.

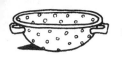   

MOM: Molly, would you show them in?

DAD: Sit down and tell us how you've been.

MOLLY: I'm glad to see you, Bobbie Dee.
Bring Puddin'head and sit by me.

GRAMPS PIERRE: Howdy do!

GRANDMA CLAIRE: How are you?

AUNTIE JANE: Hello there.

UNCLE LEE: Pull up a chair.

BUSTER: Oh, my.

BILL: Oh, me.

BLAIR: Long time, no see.

ALL: Come in, come in
and have some tea.

NARRATOR: So Grandma Claire, and Gramps Pierre,
and Buster, Bart, and Bill and Blair,
and Auntie Jane and Uncle Lee,
and Mom's young nephew, Bobbie Dee,
gave hugs and kisses all around
until they heard an awful sound.

PUDDIN'HEAD: SQUEAK-A, CREAK-A, Bobbie boy!
CRICK-A, CROAK-A, ship ahoy!

Macmillan/McGraw-Hill

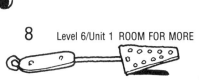  

NARRATOR: Yes, Puddin'head began to squawk
so loud that no one else could talk.
Bart began to chase Ling Shoo
and Molly wondered what to do.

MOLLY: There's no more room for us in here.
I wish that I could disappear.

MOM: Let's go outside for some fresh air.

DAD: Go out, go out and take a chair!

NARRATOR: Mom picked up the cat, Ling Shoo.
Out went Dad and Molly, too.
Grandma Claire and Gramps Pierre,
and Buster, Bart, and Bill and Blair,
and Auntie Jane and Uncle Lee,
and Puddin'head and Bobbie Dee,
all went out for some fresh air.
Each one dragged a folding chair.

Macmillan/McGraw-Hill

MOM: Everybody have a seat.
There's lots and lots of food to eat.

DAD: That's right! Dig in! It sure looks great!
Does anybody need a plate?

NARRATOR: They tasted food from France and Spain.
Not one relative complained.
As Mom served Grandma's Irish stew,
Molly smiled at what she knew.

MOLLY: We'll always welcome a new guest.
Unplanned things are often best.

MOM: There's always room for just one more.

[Knock, knock!]

MOLLY: Oh, boy! There's someone at the door!

COUSIN SUE: It's your second cousin, Sue.
I just flew in from
Kalamazoo!

GRAMPS PIERRE: Howdy do!

GRANDMA CLAIRE: How are you?

AUNTIE JANE: Hello there.

UNCLE LEE: Pull up a chair.

BUSTER: Oh, my.

BILL: Oh, me.

BLAIR: Long time, no see.

BOBBIE DEE: Have some bread.

PUDDIN'HEAD: My name is Puddin'head.

MOLLY: Come on out and take a seat.

COUSIN SUE: Seeing you is such a treat.

MOLLY: If someone knocks at our front door—

ALL: There's always room for just one more!

Macmillan/McGraw-Hill

BLOCKING DIAGRAMS

BEGINNING OF PLAY

Arrange thirteen chairs or stools, as shown. The narrator can use a music stand to hold the script.

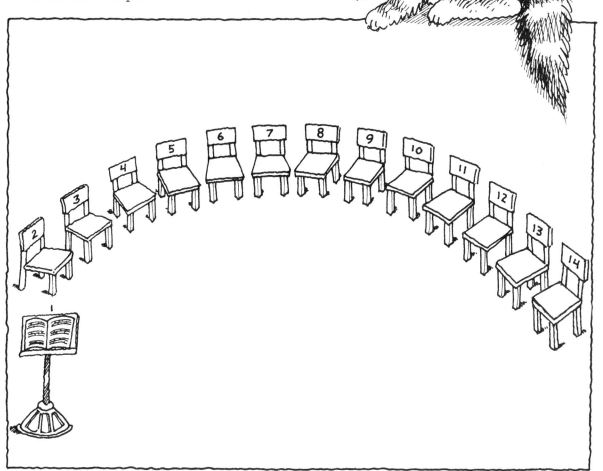

1. NARRATOR	6. MOM	11. BUSTER
2. PUDDIN'HEAD	7. DAD	12. BILL
3. BOBBIE DEE	8. MOLLY	13. BLAIR
4. AUNTIE JANE	9. GRANDMA CLAIRE	14. COUSIN SUE
5. UNCLE LEE	10. GRAMPS PIERRE	

END OF PLAY

The cast will have moved their chairs to this position.

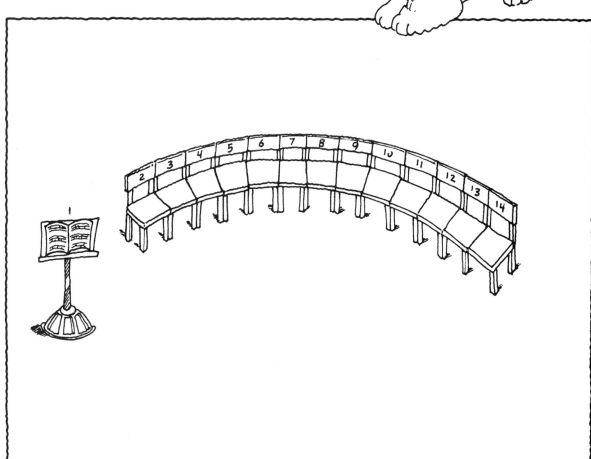

1. NARRATOR	6. MOM	11. BUSTER
2. PUDDIN'HEAD	7. DAD	12. BILL
3. BOBBIE DEE	8. MOLLY	13. BLAIR
4. AUNTIE JANE	9. GRANDMA CLAIRE	14. COUSIN SUE
5. UNCLE LEE	10. GRAMPS PIERRE	

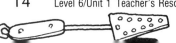

PERFORMANCE SUGGESTIONS

Much of the humor in this play stems from the crowding that takes place when one unexpected guest after another arrives. You may wish to have the children rehearse some very simple movements that will reinforce this aspect of the story after they have familiarized themselves with their parts.

Set up the chairs or stools as shown in the blocking diagram on page 13, and have the characters take their seats. Then have children begin reading *Room for More*. When Dad reads his line, "Sit down and tell us how you've been," on page 4, Grandma Claire and Gramps Pierre should stand, grasp the edge of their chairs, and slide them toward Mom, Dad, and Molly in one simple movement. After repositioning their chairs, they should sit, and Molly can resume reading. This movement should be practiced until Grandma Claire and Gramps Pierre can move in unison with as little noise as possible.

Auntie Jane and Uncle Lee repeat this action on the other side of Mom, Dad, and Molly when Dad reads the cue line, "Sit down and tell us how you've been," on page 7. This action is repeated throughout the play as each new group of characters enters and is invited to sit down. The final position of chairs will resemble the blocking diagram on page 14.

COSTUME SUGGESTIONS

Costumes for this Readers Theater production of *Room for More* should be kept to a minimum. Children can create simple costumes out of clothing, such as scarves, hats, and suit jackets, found at home. Because the children move their chairs as well as hold their scripts, purses and canes are not recommended.

A simple parrot costume can be made by attaching a few feathers, real or cut-out, to a headband and to the arms and shoulders of a colorful shirt.

Macmillan/McGraw-Hill

WHY THERE ARE NO TIGERS IN BORNEO

By Merrily P. Hansen
based on an
Indonesian folk tale

CAST

STORYTELLER

RAJAH

CHIEF MESSENGER

SECOND MESSENGER

THIRD MESSENGER

MOUSE-DEER

PORCUPINE

STORYTELLER: Far, far across the ocean, there are three islands. They are called Java, Sumatra, and Borneo. These islands are so close to each other that they could be called neighbors. Here is a surprising fact. Tigers live on Java and Sumatra. But there are no tigers at all in Borneo. Why is that, you may wonder. The people who lived on the islands also wondered why. Long, long ago, they made up a story to explain why there are no tigers in Borneo. So gather 'round, my friends, and hear the tale.

CHIEF MESSENGER: In all my years of living on Java, I can never remember weather like this. It's scorching hot!

SECOND MESSENGER: It's been weeks since we had rain. The lake beside the palace has turned into a royal puddle!

THIRD MESSENGER: All the crops in my garden have died. My family has almost nothing to eat.

STORYTELLER: The Rajah of All the Tigers, who lived on Java, knew that his subjects would die if food was not found soon. He thought and he thought. Then late one night, the rajah called three messengers to his palace and told them his plan.

RAJAH: Listen well. Take this message to the rajah of Borneo. Tell him that I demand he send food to Java. Otherwise, I will come with my army and conquer his land.

CHIEF MESSENGER: To hear is to obey, O Rajah of All the Tigers.

RAJAH: Wait. Take this with you. It is a whisker I pulled from my royal face this morning. It will show the rajah of Borneo how big and strong I am.

ALL MESSENGERS: We will guard the royal whisker with our lives.

RAJAH: Go now and return quickly with the rajah of Borneo's answer.

STORYTELLER: At dawn, the messengers left Java. They crossed the land. Then they sailed over the sea until they finally reached the island of Borneo.

CHIEF MESSENGER: Now we must search for the rajah of Borneo.

SECOND MESSENGER: I am so hot and tired from the trip. Can't we rest before we begin to look for the rajah?

THIRD MESSENGER: Look over there! Someone is spying on us!

SECOND MESSENGER: Why, it's a tiny mouse-deer hiding in the bushes.

CHIEF MESSENGER: Come here, Mouse-Deer. We have something to ask you.

MOUSE-DEER: What is it, mighty sir?

SECOND MESSENGER: We come from the Rajah of All the Tigers, who lives on Java.

THIRD MESSENGER: We have an important message to deliver to your rajah. Where is he?

MOUSE-DEER: He is hunting. What is your important message? Perhaps I can help you.

CHIEF MESSENGER: We bring word from our rajah that your rajah must surrender. Take us to your rajah so we can deliver this message.

Macmillan/McGraw-Hill

STORYTELLER: The tiny mouse-deer was a quick thinker.

MOUSE-DEER: You look so hot and tired, mighty sirs. Why don't you sit in the shade and rest? I promise to find the rajah and give him your message. Then I will bring back his answer.

SECOND MESSENGER: I *am* hot and tired. Why don't we let the mouse-deer do our running for us?

THIRD MESSENGER: Good idea. She can find her way through the forest much faster than we three.

CHIEF MESSENGER: Very well. Go, Mouse-Deer. And be quick about it! Tell your rajah that the Rajah of All the Tigers demands food.

SECOND MESSENGER: Lots of food.

THIRD MESSENGER: Enough food to feed all the tigers on Java!

CHIEF MESSENGER: Tell your rajah that the food must be given to us at once. Otherwise, our rajah will send his army to destroy you.

STORYTELLER: Then the chief messenger pulled out the huge tiger whisker and gave it to the mouse-deer.

MOUSE-DEER: What is this?

CHIEF MESSENGER: This is a whisker from the rajah's royal face. The rajah himself pulled out this whisker to show how big and brave he is.

MOUSE-DEER: It is very large. Your rajah must be strong indeed.

SECOND MESSENGER: Be off! We will wait here . . . but not too long!

STORYTELLER: The mouse-deer, holding the whisker in her mouth, ran into the forest. Her thoughts raced as she ran.

MOUSE-DEER: The rajah of Java is a tiger, and tigers eat meat. I am meat, and so are all the other animals on Borneo. If the Rajah of All the Tigers sends an army, our lives are in danger. I must think of a way to stop him.

STORYTELLER: Just then the mouse-deer heard a sound in the leaves. She saw her friend the porcupine chewing on some bark.

PORCUPINE: What's the matter, my good friend? Why are you running so fast? It's too hot to be in such a hurry.

MOUSE-DEER: I was worried . . . but seeing you has just solved my problem. I need your help, friend Porcupine.

PORCUPINE: Of course. What can I do to help?

MOUSE-DEER: Give me one of your quills. It can save Borneo for all of us.

PORCUPINE: I'll gladly give you a quill. I have more than enough. I can easily spare one quill to help Borneo.

STORYTELLER: With that, the porcupine reached around and pulled a long, sharp quill out of his tail.

MOUSE-DEER: You are a good friend, indeed. By giving this quill, you have saved our country. I'll explain everything later, but now I must be off!

STORYTELLER: The mouse-deer took the quill in her teeth and disappeared into the forest. She ran as fast as she could to the spot where the messengers from Java were waiting.

THIRD MESSENGER: Well, Mouse-Deer. It's about time.

SECOND MESSENGER: We were beginning to think that you had run away.

CHIEF MESSENGER: Did you find your rajah? Did you deliver the message?

MOUSE-DEER: O mighty ones, I am sorry I took so long. First I had to find my rajah. Then I had to wait until he woke from his nap, for he was tired after hunting.

THIRD MESSENGER: Did you tell him what our rajah said?

MOUSE-DEER: I told him everything, word for word, as you told it to me. I told him that your rajah demanded food at once, or he would come with his army and destroy us. Then I waited for his answer.

CHIEF MESSENGER: Well, what is it?

SECOND MESSENGER: What did your rajah say?

THIRD MESSENGER: Yes, yes? Speak up!

MOUSE-DEER: He said, "Very well, let the Rajah of All the Tigers in Java come and fight us."

SECOND MESSENGER: He said WHAT?

MOUSE-DEER: He said, "Let the rajah of Java come. He will find that we can fight better than he can."

THIRD MESSENGER: He said THAT?

MOUSE-DEER: In fact, his exact words were, "I am tired of peace. I would welcome a battle in which we can prove our might once more!"

CHIEF MESSENGER: Did you give him the whisker from the royal face?

MOUSE-DEER: Oh, yes, I did. And do you see this whisker?

STORYTELLER: With that, the mouse-deer held up the big, thick quill from the porcupine.

CHIEF MESSENGER: Is that a whisker?

SECOND MESSENGER: Why, it's much longer than you are!

THIRD MESSENGER: And it's thicker than your leg!

MOUSE-DEER: This whisker is from the royal face of my rajah. Here, Chief Messenger. Feel how thick and sharp it is. My rajah pulled it from his face and said I should give it to you to take back to your rajah.

STORYTELLER: The chief messenger took the whisker. He carefully felt its sharp point. His tiger stripes began to fade a bit.

CHIEF MESSENGER: Your rajah said nothing more?

MOUSE-DEER: Not one word more.

CHIEF MESSENGER: I see . . . .
Well, we must be off.

MOUSE-DEER: Oh, are you leaving?

SECOND MESSENGER: We must return at once.

THIRD MESSENGER: Our rajah is waiting for your rajah's answer.

MOUSE-DEER: Of course. I understand. It is hot here, and you have a long trip back. Be sure to take good care of my rajah's whisker.

ALL MESSENGERS: Oh, yes! You can be VERY sure of that.

MOUSE-DEER: Of course, if need be, my rajah can always send another one!

CHIEF MESSENGER: I am sure that will not be necessary. I will carry the whisker myself.

STORYTELLER: With that, the chief messenger took the big quill carefully in his paws.

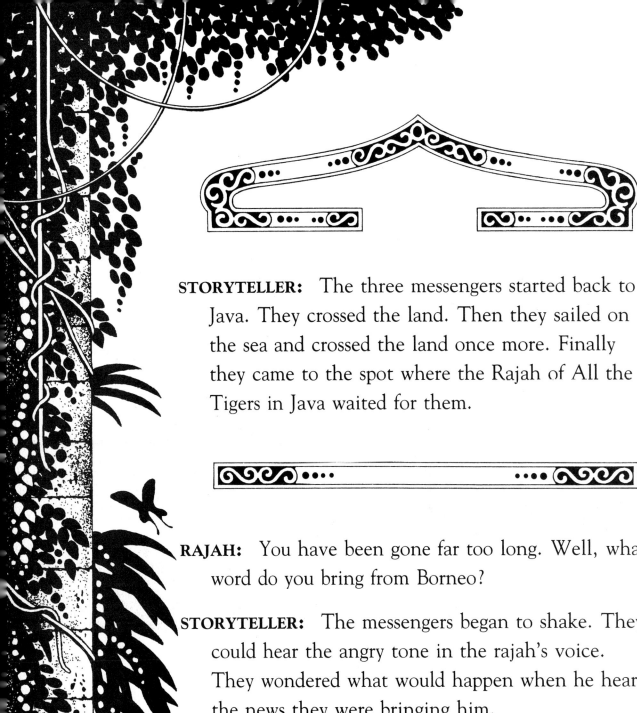

STORYTELLER: The three messengers started back to Java. They crossed the land. Then they sailed on the sea and crossed the land once more. Finally they came to the spot where the Rajah of All the Tigers in Java waited for them.

RAJAH: You have been gone far too long. Well, what word do you bring from Borneo?

STORYTELLER: The messengers began to shake. They could hear the angry tone in the rajah's voice. They wondered what would happen when he heard the news they were bringing him.

CHIEF MESSENGER: O mighty one, the miserable rajah of Borneo said he would welcome war.

RAJAH: He said he would *welcome* war?

CHIEF MESSENGER: Yes, O rajah!

RAJAH: Did you show him my royal whisker?

SECOND AND THIRD MESSENGERS: Yes, O mighty rajah.

RAJAH: What did he say?

STORYTELLER: The chief messenger stepped forward. With shaking paws he held out the big, thick porcupine quill.

CHIEF MESSENGER: He sent you this, my lord. It comes from his royal face.

STORYTELLER: The Rajah of All the Tigers in Java looked at the quill for a long time. He stroked his own whiskers all the while. He could not help feeling the difference. Then he spoke.

RAJAH: I have made a decision. I have changed my royal mind about Borneo. It would be better to demand food of the elephants of Sumatra.

STORYTELLER: Whether the elephants of Sumatra ever sent the food, the story does not tell. But it is a fact that from that day to this, there have been no tigers in Borneo.

Blocking ◆ Diagram

Arrange seven chairs or stools, as shown.

1. NARRATOR
2. RAJAH OF ALL THE TIGERS
3. CHIEF MESSENGER
4. SECOND MESSENGER

5. THIRD MESSENGER
6. MOUSE-DEER
7. PORCUPINE

Indonesia

Indonesia is made up of more than 5,000 islands. They stretch almost 3,000 miles along the equator. That is just about the length of the United States from its east coast to its west coast.

There are many different kinds of animals in Indonesia. You can see crocodiles, snakes, and colorful birds on all the islands. There are elephants in Sumatra and Borneo, and tigers in Java. But as the play tells us, there are no tigers in Borneo.

The islands are full of forests, volcanoes, mountains, and rivers, and everything has its own story. The storyteller is a very important person in the village. Puppet shows help tell the stories to both children and adults.

Where • in • the • World?

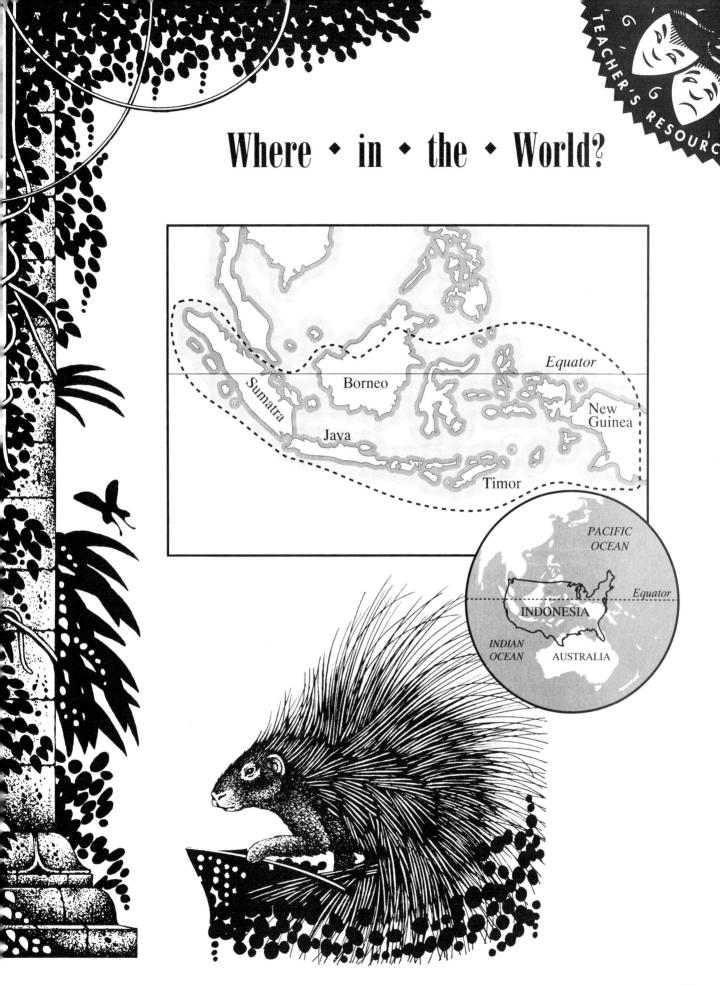

Sumatra

Borneo

Equator

New Guinea

Java

Timor

PACIFIC OCEAN

Equator

INDONESIA

INDIAN OCEAN

AUSTRALIA

TEACHER'S RESOURCE

Shadow • Puppet • Play
Directions

In Indonesia, shadow plays are the most popular form of theater. In this type of puppet show, the puppeteer manipulates puppets behind a thin screen made of paper or fabric while a strong light casts the shadows of the puppets onto the screen.

Here is an easy and inexpensive way to make a theater for a shadow puppet play.

1. Start with a large corrugated appliance box, such as a refrigerator carton. If a large box is not available, use a smaller box placed on a desk or table. Another alternative is to use a doorway.

2. Cut away one side of the box, leaving a three-sided screen. Then cut a window in the upper part of the center panel. Make the opening high enough to allow the children to stand or sit comfortably without their heads or hands casting a shadow on the screen.

Macmillan/McGraw-Hill

Shadow • Puppet • Play
Directions

3. For the screen, choose a piece of thin, opaque white fabric, such as an old white sheet, a large sheet of translucent tracing paper, or rice paper. Keep the fabric or paper as taut as possible when fastening it to the window opening. If a doorway is used, stretch the fabric across the top portion of the opening. Conceal the puppeteers with a sheet of opaque paper taped across the bottom.

4. Place a slide projector or a gooseneck lamp with a strong bulb behind the screen for lighting. An exciting effect can be created by projecting a slide of a forest on the screen. A little experimentation will help children determine the most effective distance and height for the light. Then it's on with the show!

Shadow ◆ Puppets

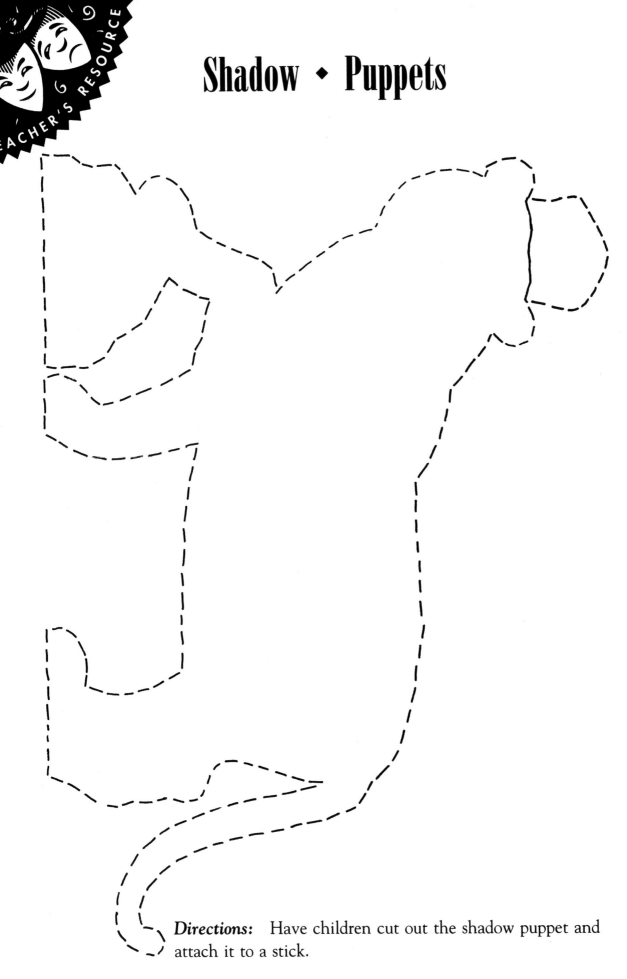

Directions: Have children cut out the shadow puppet and attach it to a stick.

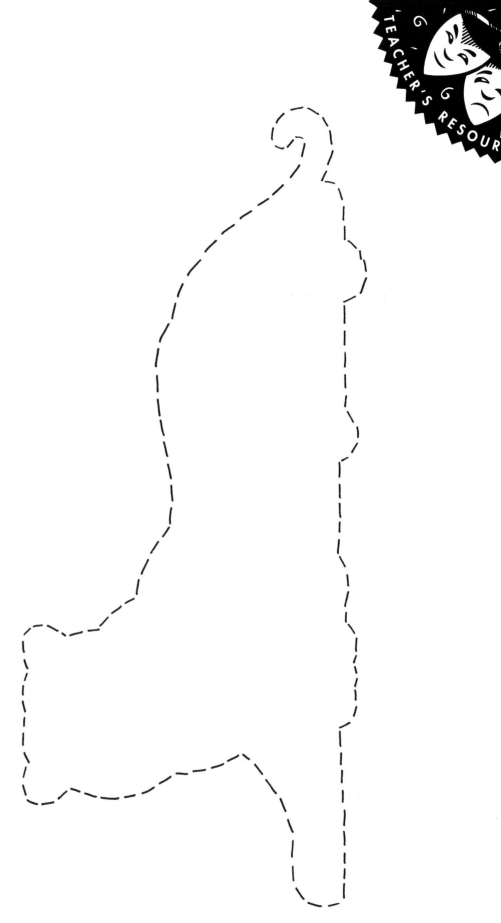

Directions: Have children cut out the shadow puppet and attach it to a stick.

Directions: Have children cut out the shadow puppet and attach it to a stick.

Macmillan/McGraw-Hill

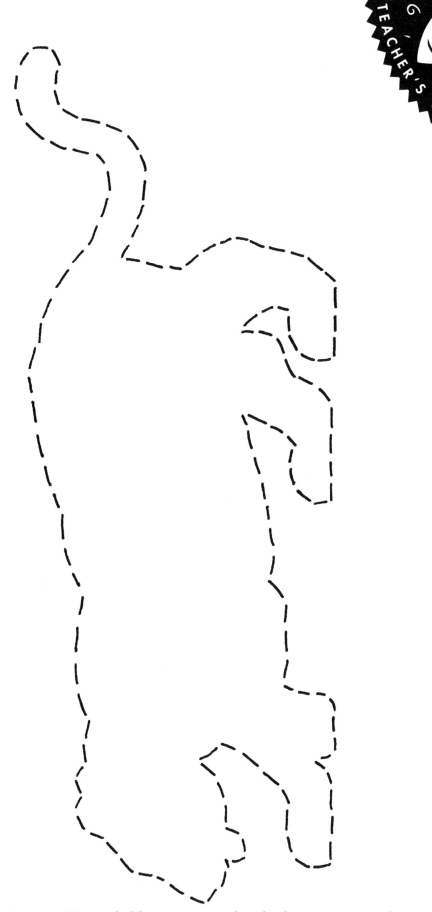

Directions: Have children cut out the shadow puppet and attach it to a stick.

Directions: Have children cut out the shadow puppet and attach it to a stick.

Macmillan/McGraw-Hill

A WHALE of A STORY

Judith Bauer Stamper

CAST:
NED BROWN, News Anchor
GWEN HILLMAN, News Reporter
LISA PERINI, Marine Biologist
GREGG CRUZ, 7-Year-Old Boy
JENNY LUCAS, 9-Year-Old Girl
CAPTAIN WILLS, Coast Guard Captain
SAM JONES, Fisherman
CHRIS JACOBS, Bridge Engineer

Macmillan/McGraw-Hill

NED BROWN: Good evening, I'm Ned Brown. And this is Spotlight News. Today, our top story is Humphrey, the humpback whale. Humphrey swam into San Francisco Bay over two weeks ago. And ever since, Humphrey has been going the wrong way! He's now sixty miles from the ocean, and in trouble—*very big trouble*. Our reporter, Gwen Hillman, is with Humphrey near the Liberty Island Bridge. Gwen, can you hear me?

GWEN HILLMAN: Yes, Ned. I'm here, along with hundreds of Humphrey fans. They're all hoping to catch sight of their favorite whale.

NED BROWN: Fill us in on what's going on there, Gwen.

GWEN HILLMAN: I'm standing only a few feet from the Liberty Island Bridge, Ned. For more than a week now, this bridge has held Humphrey a prisoner. He's got to go under it to get to the ocean. But he can't find a big enough space to swim through. Yesterday, he made several tries. But each time, he turned back.

NED BROWN: Humphrey did swim under that bridge to get to where he is now, didn't he?

GWEN HILLMAN: That's right. Somehow he managed to squeeze through. But now he can't seem to find his way back out. Someone here said it's like being in a dark cave with a lot of passages. Think how hard it would be to find your way out.

NED BROWN: That sounds serious for Humphrey.

GWEN HILLMAN: It is, Ned. There're a lot of worried people here. They wonder how much longer Humphrey can survive. Let's talk to a few of them now. This is Lisa Perini, a scientist who's an expert on whales. Lisa, can you tell us how Humphrey is feeling?

LISA PERINI: Humphrey is in trouble, and I think he knows it. From watching him, I would say that this whale is stressed out.

GWEN HILLMAN: Just what do you mean by that, Lisa?

LISA PERINI: Look out over the water. I think he's going to do it again. Yes, there he goes, smacking his huge tail against the water.

GWEN HILLMAN: That made quite a splash! But what does it mean?

LISA PERINI: Humphrey is trying to signal other whales. He's smacking his tail to ask for help. That's what whales do in the ocean. But no other whales are around to hear or see him.

GWEN HILLMAN: Do you think Humphrey wants to get back to the ocean, Lisa?

LISA PERINI: Without a doubt, Gwen. Just think, Humphrey is a forty-ton whale. Right now he's trying to swim in water that's only ten feet deep in places! He must be scraping his belly on the bottom at times. And that has to hurt!

GWEN HILLMAN: Can a whale like Humphrey live in this water, Lisa? Isn't he used to ocean salt water?

LISA PERINI: Good point, Gwen. Whales belong in salt water. We're worried about what this fresh river water might do to Humphrey. It may be seeping through his skin. That could cause real problems. Before long, Humphrey could get waterlogged!

GWEN HILLMAN: What are Humphrey's chances of making it out of here alive, Lisa?

LISA PERINI: I think he can still make it, but this bridge is holding him back. Humphrey needs to get back to salt water—and soon!

GWEN HILLMAN: Thank you, Lisa. Back to you, Ned.

NED BROWN: What about all the children there, Gwen? How do they feel about Humphrey?

GWEN HILLMAN: Here's a boy right now wearing a Save-the-Whale T-shirt. Excuse me, could you answer a few questions? First tell us your name.

GREGG CRUZ: I'm . . . um . . . Gregg Cruz. Am I really on television?

GWEN HILLMAN: Yes, you are, Gregg.

GREGG CRUZ: Wow!

GWEN HILLMAN: Gregg, I see you are a fan of Humphrey's. What do you think will happen today?

GREGG CRUZ: I hope he gets free! I come here every day on my bike to see him. It's almost like having a pet whale. But I know he's got to get back to the ocean. They have to find some way to help Humphrey.

GWEN HILLMAN: Thanks, Gregg. Here's another young person who looks interested in Humphrey. What's your name?

JENNY LUCAS: I'm Jenny Lucas.

GWEN HILLMAN: Well, Jenny. What do you think of Humphrey?

JENNY LUCAS: I think Humphrey is the most exciting thing I've ever seen. A real humpback whale in our own backyard! Humphrey has made me care about the whales more than I ever did before. You know, there are only about ten thousand humpback whales left in the whole world! So we just can't let this one die!

Macmillan/McGraw-Hill

GWEN HILLMAN: Thanks, Jenny. You know, a lot of people are doing everything they can to save Humphrey. I see one of them right now, Coast Guard Captain Michael Wills. You are working to protect Humphrey, aren't you, Captain Wills?

CAPTAIN WILLS: That's right, Gwen. Right now, the Coast Guard is doing its best to protect Humphrey from the boaters on the river.

GWEN HILLMAN: Did you say from the *boaters,* Captain? What do you mean?

CAPTAIN WILLS: Lots of people wanted a close-up view of this whale. They were running their motorboats right up to him. Poor Humphrey was scared by the sound of their engines.

GWEN HILLMAN: What have you done to stop the boaters, Captain Wills?

CAPTAIN WILLS: We've told them to clear out of the area. If necessary, we're ready to back up our words with action. That means up to a twenty-thousand-dollar fine!

GWEN HILLMAN: I'm sure the boaters are just curious. But they do have to think of Humphrey first. Ned, do you have any questions for Captain Wills?

NED BROWN: First of all, thank you for taking the time to speak with us today, Captain Wills.

CAPTAIN WILLS: You're welcome, Ned. I'm a big fan of yours.

NED BROWN: Captain Wills, I'm hoping you can clear something up. We've been getting reports that the Coast Guard is banging on underwater pipes. Doesn't that scare Humphrey?

CAPTAIN WILLS: As you know, Ned, whales are very sensitive to underwater sounds. Our hope is that Humphrey will swim away from the banging sounds toward the ocean.

NED BROWN: But where did you get the idea of banging on pipes?

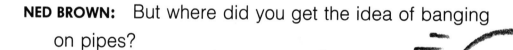

Macmillan/McGraw-Hill

CAPTAIN WILLS: From Japanese fishermen, Ned. They bang on pipes to drive dolphins from their fishing nets. Yesterday, we tried doing the same thing with Humphrey.

NED BROWN: And how did it work, Captain Wills?

CAPTAIN WILLS: Everything was going according to plan—until Humphrey reached the bridge. Then he stopped. Our feeling is that he's more frightened of the bridge than the pipes. We had to stop the banging because we didn't want to upset him.

GWEN HILLMAN: Thank you, Captain. Ned, as you may have seen on camera, Humphrey slapped his tail on the water again just seconds ago. There was a roar of excitement from this crowd. Here's someone right now who seems to want to say something. Hello, what's your name?

SAM JONES: I'm Sam Jones. I own a fishing boat. And I've been fishing around these parts for years.

GWEN HILLMAN: That's very interesting, Mr. Jones. And what would you like to share with our viewers?

SAM JONES: I'd just like to say that not enough has been done to save that whale.

GWEN HILLMAN: What do you suggest, Mr. Jones?

SAM JONES: I say we should lift him right out of the water with a helicopter. He wouldn't have to swim under the bridge. He could fly right over it!

GWEN HILLMAN: Really, Mr. Jones. Isn't that a little farfetched? How could you lift a whale by helicopter?

SAM JONES: Why, you could just put some straps around him and lift him right up.

GWEN HILLMAN: Well, Ned, that's just one of the ideas that people have come up with to save Humphrey. I wonder if Mr. Jones remembers that Humphrey weighs 40 tons and is 45 feet long. And I don't think he would let anybody put straps around him!

LISA PERINI: Excuse me, Gwen, but I just heard that man talking. That's not the only wild idea we've heard! Somebody else wanted to drop a trail of salt cubes in the river. Humphrey was supposed to follow them out to sea! That idea would never work. The salt would kill the plants and animals that live in the river.

GWEN HILLMAN: People care about Humphrey and want to help, but they just don't know what might work and what won't. Ned, do you have something you want to add?

NED BROWN: Just an interesting number. Over ten thousand people have called in with ideas about how to save Humphrey. But they've got to let the experts do the work.

GWEN HILLMAN: I have one of those experts here with me right now. This is Chris Jacobs. He's the engineer who has been working to help Humphrey get under the bridge. Hello, Chris.

CHRIS JACOBS: Hello, Gwen. I'm glad you're here with your crew because something exciting is going to happen any minute.

GWEN HILLMAN: What do you mean, Chris?

CHRIS JACOBS: We've been working on this bridge since yesterday. In fact, we worked all through the night, cleaning out the old wood and garbage on the river bottom. It was blocking the space between the wood pilings that hold up the bridge. Underwater, those pilings must have looked like shark's teeth to poor Humphrey! I'm hoping that today he'll make it through.

GWEN HILLMAN: I can see the boats out there right now. It looks as if they're trying to drive Humphrey toward the bridge. I can hear them banging on the underwater pipes again.

JENNY LUCAS: Look! There's Humphrey! He's swimming in the direction of the bridge.

GREGG CRUZ: Come on, Humphrey. You can do it!

SAM JONES: Go, Humphrey, go! Don't let that bridge stop you. You've got to get back to the ocean!

GWEN HILLMAN: Ned, the excitement is building up. People are standing on both sides of the river. They're watching Humphrey make another try to get under the bridge. Will he make it? Lisa, what do you think his chances are?

LISA PERINI: I don't know, Gwen. But, look! Humphrey is getting closer and closer to the bridge. I just saw his back come out of the water. He's diving! He's trying to dive under the bridge!

CHRIS JACOBS: Oh no, he's stuck! I can see one of his fins. It's caught between two of the wood pilings.

JENNY LUCAS: Can't somebody do something! What's going to happen to Humphrey?

GWEN HILLMAN: Ned, the crowd is holding its breath. This is a very dangerous moment for Humphrey. Lisa, what do you think the whale will do?

LISA PERINI: He's going to do everything he can to free himself. But I don't know if he'll be able to. Wait! Humphrey seems to be sinking! I can't see him anymore. He's sinking to the bottom of the river.

GWEN HILLMAN: Ned, the suspense is unbelievable. No one knows what's happened to Humphrey. Is he hurt? Is he resting? Wait, I see him coming out of the water! He's lifting one fin into the air. And he's squeezing through those two pilings.

GREGG CRUZ: Go, Humphrey, go!

JENNY LUCAS: You can do it, Humphrey!

SAM JONES: That's the way, Humphrey!

GWEN HILLMAN: He's done it! Humphrey's made it through the bridge! You can hear the people around here cheering. They are wild with excitement!

CHRIS JACOBS: He's going to be all right! I can see him on the other side of the bridge. And he's finally headed in the right direction—back to the ocean.

GWEN HILLMAN: What do you think, Lisa? Is Humphrey on his way home at last? Will he have enough strength to make it to the Pacific Ocean?

LISA PERINI: Gwen, I just got a good look at him when he came up out of the water. His skin seems to be in good shape. Humphrey also showed a lot of strength getting through those bridge pilings. I think he'll be all right.

GWEN HILLMAN: Captain Wills, I know you're going to have to get back to your boat soon. What is your next step in saving Humphrey?

CAPTAIN WILLS: We'll try to keep Humphrey headed down the river. Instead of banging on the pipes, we'll start to use some tapes of the sounds whales make when they're feeding.

LISA PERINI: Let's just hope that Humphrey is hungry enough to follow these sounds right out to the ocean!

GWEN HILLMAN: Did you hear that roar of laughter, Ned? Humphrey just blew a fountain of water into the air. I think he's on his way home.

NED BROWN: This has been a great moment in a whale of a story. Thank you, Gwen. We'll be back later for an update on Humphrey as he makes his way back to the ocean. For now, that's all from Spotlight News.

Setting the Stage for Videotaping

Place chairs for the actors and the crew as shown.

The floor manager holds up the cue cards, and the sound effects person provides sound effects at the appropriate times.

TYPES OF VIDEOTAPE SHOTS

MEDIUM SHOT

CLOSE-UP

WIDE SHOT

Videotaping the Play

VIDEO VOCABULARY

pan	move the camera slowly left or right
fast pan	move the camera quickly left or right
zoom in	move the lens toward the subject to make the subject larger
zoom out	move the lens away to make the subject smaller
voice-over	a voice is heard, but the speaker is not seen

GENERAL HINTS FOR SHOOTING A VIDEO PLAY

✔ Before you begin the actual videotaping, test the sound level. Since you'll be using the built-in camera microphone, it is best to stand no more than 8 to 10 feet away from the actors. During the taping, use the earpiece that comes with the camera to make sure that the children can be heard. If their voices are too soft, move in closer.

✔ If you stop the camera between shots, be sure to wait one or two seconds after restarting the camera before cueing the speaker to begin.

SHOOTING THE PLAY

✔ Page 45: Begin with a medium shot of Ned in the studio. Then fast pan to Gwen. After his first speech, Ned should leave the studio and stand next to the camera. He will do voice-overs from this position until after his speech on page 55.

✔ Page 45: When Gwen is speaking to Ned, use a medium shot of Gwen or zoom in for a close-up. Gwen should look directly at the camera when she talks to Ned.

Macmillan/McGraw-Hill

✔ Page 46: Gwen should extend the mike toward Lisa Perini. When Gwen turns to Lisa, zoom out to a wide shot. Follow this procedure with subsequent interviews. For variety, after Gwen introduces the person being interviewed, zoom in on that person. Keep the close-up throughout the interview. Then go back to the wide shot for Gwen's final comment.

✔ Page 55: After Ned reads his lines on this page, he should return to the studio.

✔ Page 60: Fast pan from Gwen to the studio for Ned's closing remarks.

✔ Page 60: To close the show, press the fade-out button or pass your hand directly in front of the lens, top to bottom. Then stop the camera.

Sound Effects

EQUIPMENT AND DIRECTIONS

Sound effects add realism to *A Whale of a Story,* and they're fun to do. The children will need a few props and some cue cards.

PROPS   **CUE CARDS**

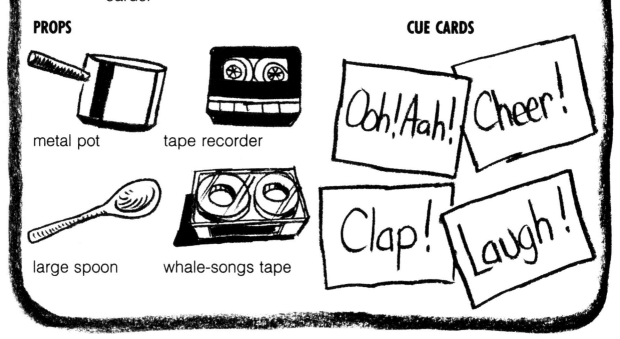

metal pot   tape recorder

large spoon   whale-songs tape

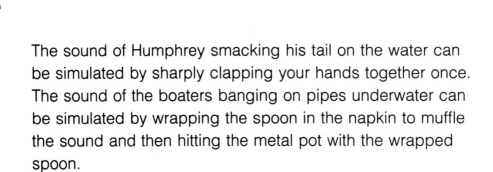

The sound of Humphrey smacking his tail on the water can be simulated by sharply clapping your hands together once. The sound of the boaters banging on pipes underwater can be simulated by wrapping the spoon in the napkin to muffle the sound and then hitting the metal pot with the wrapped spoon.

THE SCRIPT

Sound effects will be needed on the script pages listed below. Both the sound-effects person and the floor manager should note the sound effects in their scripts.

page 46, after line 21   sound effect: slap of Humphrey's tail

cue card:

Ooh! Aah!

page 53, before line 11   sound effect: slap of Humphrey's tail

cue card:

Ooh! Aah!

page 57, after line 4   sound effect: banging on pipes

page 58, after line 17   cue cards:

Cheer!

Clap!

page 60, after line 7   cue cards:

Cheer!

Laugh!

page 60, after line 14   sound effect: whale-songs tape

THE PERFORMANCE

Arrange the sound-effects props and a script that has the sound effects marked on it on a desk facing the actors, as shown on page 61.

Place the cue cards on another desk for the floor manager's use. Explain to the children in the audience that they will provide the crowd reactions called for in the play. The floor manager will silently prompt them by using the cue cards. He or she will also use hand signals to direct them.

SOFTER   **LOUDER**   **STOP! CUT!**

Props

✔ To create a backdrop for Gwen Hillman, have the children make a mural on butcher paper or on the chalkboard. The scene should include the Liberty Island Bridge with its pilings, crowds of people and many cars on the riverbanks, Humphrey partially submerged near the bridge, and two or three Coast Guard boats.

✔ To allow the children to simulate videotaping *A Whale of a Story,* make a video camera from a shoebox or cereal box painted gray or white. For the lens, insert a 3- or 4-inch cardboard tube from a roll of paper towels into one narrow end of the box.

 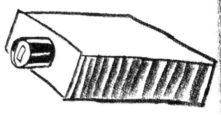

✔ The camera operator can wear an actual headset from a portable radio or cassette-tape player or a pair of earmuffs covered with black cloth.

✔ Attach a black yarn "cable" to a small spring-clamp and clip it on Ned's shirt for his body mike.

✔ To make Gwen's microphone, begin with the cardboard tube from a roll of paper towels. Cut an 8- or 9-inch length of tube. Cover a small ball, such as a Ping-Pong ball, with aluminum foil and tape it to the open end of the tube. Tape a few yards of black yarn inside the opposite end of the mike, and the crew is ready to roll tape.

by Joe Claro

CAST

MOTHER GOOSE

HUMPTY DUMPTY

KING COLE

JACK HORNER

COW

WILLIE WINKIE

TOMMY TUCKER

MISS MUFFET

Macmillan/McGraw-Hill

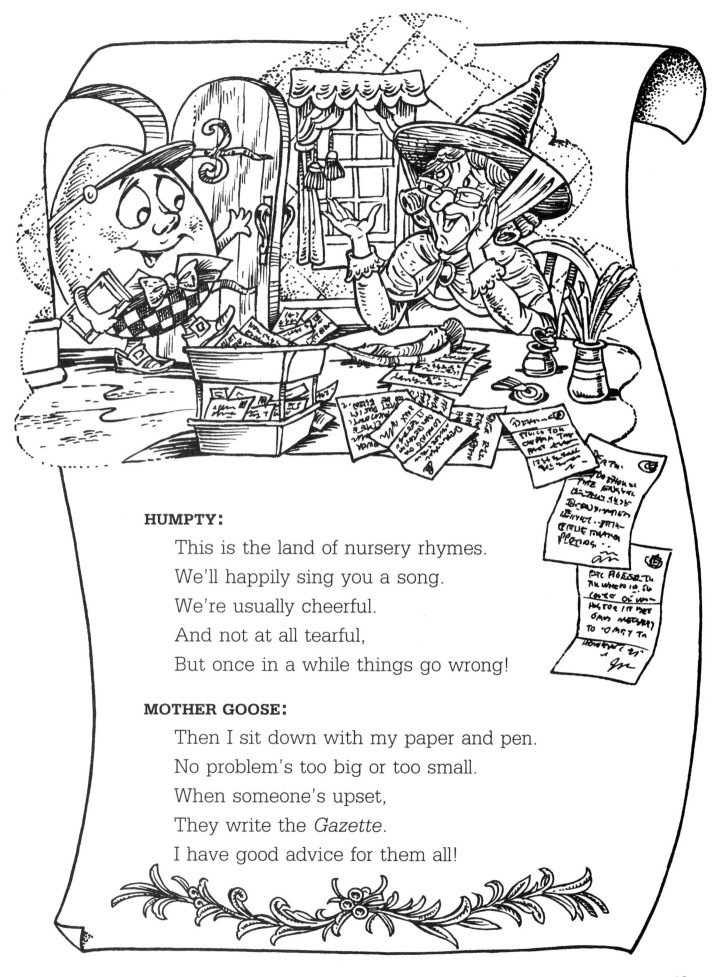

HUMPTY:

This is the land of nursery rhymes.

We'll happily sing you a song.

We're usually cheerful.

And not at all tearful,

But once in a while things go wrong!

MOTHER GOOSE:

Then I sit down with my paper and pen.

No problem's too big or too small.

When someone's upset,

They write the *Gazette*.

I have good advice for them all!

HUMPTY: Morning, Mother Goose. Here's your mail.

MOTHER GOOSE: Good morning, Humpty Dumpty. Oh, I do love getting all this mail! I'm so glad I switched from the Giving-Out-Jobs Department to the Giving-Out-Advice Department. Well, let's get to work. What do we have today?

HUMPTY: Here's a letter right on top from someone named Cole.

MOTHER GOOSE: Cole? Cole? Oh, yes, I remember. I found him a job as a king. Do we have a copy of that poem I wrote for him? It's been a while.

HUMPTY: Here it is, Mother Goose.

Old King Cole
    Was a merry old soul,
And a merry old soul was he;
    He called for his pipe,
    And he called for his bowl,
    And he called for his fiddlers three.

MOTHER GOOSE: Thank you, Humpty. What does King Cole say in his letter?

KING COLE:

Dear Mother Goose,

I have a problem, and I hope you can help. This morning I was sitting on my throne being merry, as usual. I decided to call for my pipe, and a page brought it to me. Then I called for my bowl. Another page brought me one filled to the top with sweet red cherries.

MOTHER GOOSE: That sounds nice. Old King Cole certainly has a pleasant life. What kind of problem could he have?

KING COLE:

> Everything was going just fine. Then I called for my fiddlers three. Fiddler One came in and played a snappy tune. Next, Fiddler Two came in and played a lovely waltz. Then Fiddler Three arrived. And that's when my problem began.

MOTHER GOOSE: Oh, good! A problem! Now he's going to ask me for advice.

KING COLE:

> It was time for my nap, so Fiddler Three started to play "Rock-a-bye Baby." Screech! Screech! Screech! His fiddle sounded as squeaky as my old suit of armor! No one could sleep through that racket. What am I to do? I need my afternoon nap!
>
> Sleepily, *King Cole*

MOTHER GOOSE: Oh, how sad! Poor King Cole. Humpty, I'll dictate a letter and you write it. We'll print it in the afternoon edition of the *Gazette*.

HUMPTY: Go ahead. I'm ready.

MOTHER GOOSE:

Dear King Cole,

    I'm sorry to hear about your troubles. However, there's a simple answer. All you have to do is get a pair of earmuffs. Put them on and let Fiddler Three screech away. You won't hear a thing. Try it. You'll be asleep in no time at all.

    Helpfully yours, **MOTHER GOOSE**

HUMPTY: Excuse me, Mother Goose. Do you *really* think this is good advice?

MOTHER GOOSE: Of course it is! King Cole will be very grateful. Now, who sent the next letter?

HUMPTY: It's from one of the cows who used to work at the Rhymeland Dairy. Here's the poem you wrote for her:

> Hey, diddle-diddle,
> The cat and the fiddle,
> The cow jumped over the moon;
> The little dog laughed
> To see such sport,
> And the dish ran away with the spoon.

MOTHER GOOSE: My, my. That cow is one of the most talented athletes in Rhymeland. Let's hear her letter.

Macmillan/McGraw-Hill

COW:

Dear Mother Goose,

Well, I did what you said in the rhyme you wrote for me. Now here I am, orbiting the earth. I don't like it up here. I'm the only cow in the neighborhood. How can I get back down to the dairy, where I belong?

Going around in circles,

THE COW

MOTHER GOOSE: Oh, my, that *is* a problem. Humpty, please take down this reply:

Dear Cow,

I must be honest with you. I never thought you'd be lonely in the Milky Way. But I do have a suggestion. As you orbit, watch for Rhymeland. When you see it, swish your tail back and forth as fast as you can. That should bring you back down to earth. See you soon.

Your friend,

MOTHER GOOSE

HUMPTY: Something tells me we won't be seeing her as soon as you think. This next letter is from Jack Horner. He lives behind the Rhymeland Bakery, remember? Here's the rhyme you wrote for him.

Little Jack Horner
Sat in the corner,
Eating a Christmas pie;
He put in his thumb,
And pulled out a plum,
And said, "What a good boy am I!"

MOTHER GOOSE: And he is a very good boy indeed. What's troubling him?

JACK HORNER:

Dear Mother Goose:

I've been doing the job you assigned me every day for six months. I now have plums everywhere! I've got plums in the kitchen, plums in the basement, and plums in my closet. My garage is filled with plums. Please tell me what to do! Fast!

Worriedly,

JACK HORNER

MOTHER GOOSE: That boy does need my advice! Humpty, please write down this answer:

> Dear Jack,
> From now on, after you've pulled out a plum, simply eat it. As for your present problem, there's only one solution.
> Move immediately!
>
> Your friend,
>
> **MOTHER GOOSE**
>
> P.S. I hear Mother Hubbard has a bare cupboard. You could take some plums over to her place.

HUMPTY: This next letter is from that boy with the night job. Here's his rhyme.

> Wee Willie Winkie
> runs through the town,
> Upstairs and downstairs,
> in his nightgown,
> Rapping at the window,
> crying through the lock,
> "Are the children in their beds?
> Now it's eight o'clock."

Macmillan/McGraw-Hill

WILLIE:

Dear Mother Goose,

I'm writing because I need your advice. You see, I sleep during the day and I work at night. I go around to make sure all the children in Rhymeland are in bed by eight o'clock.

MOTHER GOOSE: I'm sure their parents like that. What could be wrong?

WILLIE:

Now, here's my problem. I set my alarm clock for seven o'clock at night. That gives me just enough time to get up and brush my teeth before I go out and rap on windows and rattle locks. But my alarm clock just broke, and I'm afraid I'll oversleep. What should I do?

Alarmingly yours,

Wee Willie Winkie

MOTHER GOOSE: Poor little lad. He has a perfect on-time record. No wonder he's worried. Humpty, please take this down:

Dear Willie,

    Your problem is a simple one. And it has a simple solution. Get a rooster. Put him on your night table. Ask the rooster to stand on his head. By doing this, he will do everything backwards. Instead of crowing at seven o'clock in the morning, he'll crow at seven o'clock at night. See? I told you it was simple.

    Helpfully yours,

MOTHER GOOSE

HUMPTY: Now we move on to a letter from Little Tommy Tucker. Remember him? He's the boy with the golden voice.

> Little Tommy Tucker
>> Sings for his supper:
> What shall we give him?
>> White bread and butter.

MOTHER GOOSE: Of course I remember Tommy. He's hoping to make TV commercials. What does he have to say?

TOMMY:

Dear Mother Goose,

   It's been a great year. I've been singing for my supper every night. And every night I get that white bread and butter that I love so much. Now here's my problem. I woke up this morning with a sore throat. The doctor told me not to sing until it gets better. What should I do?

   Musically yours,

   LITTLE TOMMY TUCKER

MOTHER GOOSE: Humpty, please take this down:

> Dear Tommy,
>   Gargle.
>   Healthfully yours,
>
>
>
> **MOTHER GOOSE**
>
> P.S.   You really should try to cut down on the butter. All that fat isn't good for you.

HUMPTY: Maybe he ought to try some soup. Here's the last letter, Mother Goose. It's from Little Miss Muffet.

> Little Miss Muffet
> Sat on a tuffet,
> Eating her curds and whey;
> There came a big spider,
> Who sat down beside her
> And frightened Miss Muffet away.

MOTHER GOOSE: Poor thing. I can't believe I made up that job for such a sweet, young girl! What does Miss Muffet have to say?

MISS MUFFET:

Dear Mother Goose,
    You'll be happy to know that because of this job, I'm doing very well in my science class. I know more about spiders than anyone else at school.

MOTHER GOOSE: Oh, I was so right to give her that job!

MISS MUFFET:

    But I have a problem. Actually, I have *two* problems. The first is with my curds and whey. I know they both come from milk. But I can't remember which is which. I'm afraid I may be eating my whey and curds, instead of my curds and whey.

MOTHER GOOSE: Oh, my. And what's her second problem?

MISS MUFFET:

My second problem is that tuffet. Could you please tell me what a tuffet is? I can't sit on one unless I know what it *is!*

Curiously,

LITTLE MISS MUFFET

HUMPTY: I've often wondered what a tuffet is. And I don't know what curds and whey are, either. What reply do you want me to print, Mother Goose?

MOTHER GOOSE: Reply? What do you mean?

HUMPTY: Why, a reply to Little Miss Muffet's letter. Aren't you going to answer her questions?

MOTHER GOOSE: H-m-m-m. I don't think so.

HUMPTY: Why, Mother Goose! You don't know the answers, do you? You wrote the poem, but you don't know what a tuffet is.

MOTHER GOOSE: Well, I do know that *tuffet* rhymes with *Muffet*. And that's what counts when you're writing nursery rhymes!

Macmillan/McGraw-Hill

HUMPTY: And how about curds and whey?

MOTHER GOOSE: I did know the difference once. But that was a long time ago.

HUMPTY: So, what should we tell Little Miss Muffet?

MOTHER GOOSE: I don't know. Wait! I've got it! We'll solve her problems by giving her a new job.

HUMPTY: What do you mean?

MOTHER GOOSE: Miss Muffet's first name is Mary, isn't it?

HUMPTY: Why, yes. I think it is.

MOTHER GOOSE: Wonderful! Miss Muffet said she's doing well in her science class. That means she must like school. Well, I've been working on a rhyme about a lamb that follows a girl named Mary to school. Let's bring Miss Muffet into the office and talk to her about this new job.

HUMPTY: Okay. I'll call her. Then I'll drop these letters off at the printer's shop.

MOTHER GOOSE: Thank you, Humpty.

HUMPTY: Right! See you later.

MOTHER GOOSE:

Here in the land of nursery rhymes,
Things often go wrong, as you see.
Got a problem or two?
I know just what to do.
So relax, and leave it to me!

BLOCKING DIAGRAM

Arrange eight chairs or stools, as shown.

1. KING COLE
2. JACK HORNER
3. TOMMY TUCKER
4. HUMPTY DUMPTY
5. MOTHER GOOSE
6. MISS MUFFET
7. WILLIE WINKIE
8. COW

TEACHER'S RESOURCE

Macmillan/McGraw-Hill

Directions: Color and cut out the hat parts. Tape them together. Glue to a headband. The picture shows you how.

Directions: Have children color and cut out the hat patterns.
Attach them to headbands, as shown in the illustration.

Directions: Have children color and cut out the hat pattern. Attach it to a headband, as shown in the illustration.

Directions: Have children color and cut out the hat pattern. Attach it to a headband, as shown in the illustration.

Directions: Have children color and cut out the hat pattern. Attach it to a headband, as shown in the illustration.

Macmillan/McGraw-Hill

Directions: Have children color and cut out the hat pattern.

Attach it to a headband, as shown in the illustration.

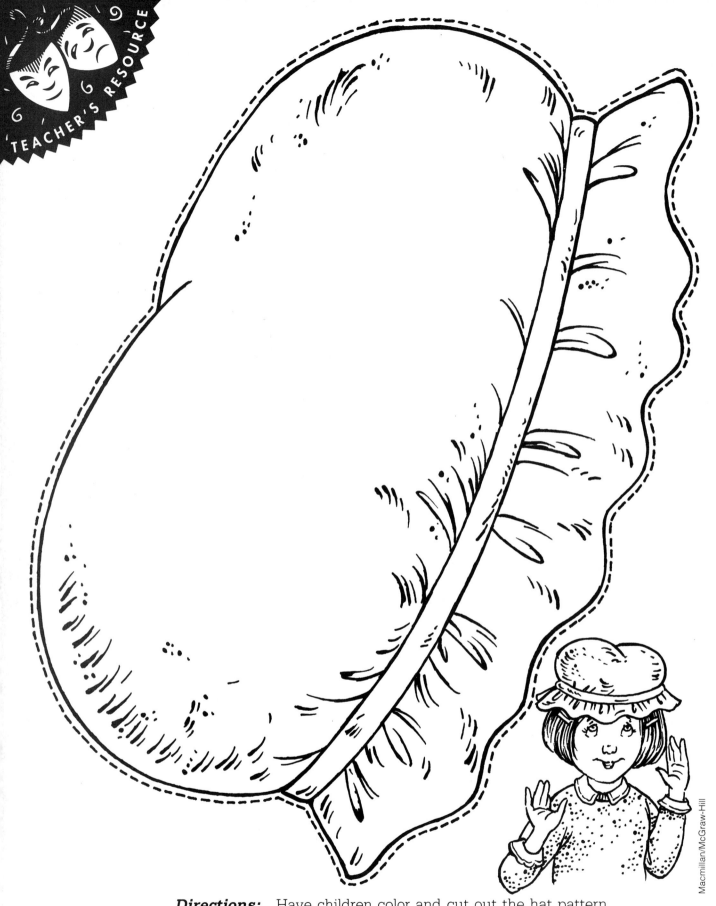

Directions: Have children color and cut out the hat pattern.
Attach it to a headband, as shown in the illustration.

I'LL BE THE DRAGON!

KATHLEEN M. FISCHER

CAST:

JANE *(Narrator)*   WILLIAM *(Witch)*

ARTHUR *(Farmer)*   SARAH *(Bird)*

RHODA *(Dragon)*   JOSH *(Blacksmith)*

ACT I

JANE: Once upon a time, not so very long ago, some second graders were rehearsing a Readers Theater play.

ARTHUR: Hey! Have you guys read this play about the dragon? It's going to be great!

RHODA: You bet! I just *love* plays about dragons.

WILLIAM: Yeah! Dragon plays are almost as good as monster plays.

SARAH: Well, if you ask me, the first thing we should do is pick our parts. Has everyone read the play?

ALL (except Sarah): YES!

JOSH: The dragon seems like kind of a sad character. We need someone who can sound sad and not very scary.

WILLIAM: I can be the dragon. I can really roar. Just listen to this: R-R-R-ROAR!

ARTHUR: Wait a minute! Dragons don't roar. Besides, this play doesn't have that kind of dragon. He's not a monster. He's sort of nice, really. We need someone who can sound friendly and helpful. Someone like *me,* for instance.

SARAH: But Arthur, the dragon has to be able to solve people's problems. I'm a great problem solver. I think *I* should play the dragon.

JOSH: Well, everybody knows a dragon should be played by a boy. *I'll* be the dragon.

JANE: Not so fast! A girl can be a very good dragon. As a matter of fact, *I* would be perfect!

RHODA: Listen, I don't want to hurt anyone's feelings, but *I* was sort of hoping to play the dragon.

WILLIAM: Hold on! I'm the scariest one here. I still say *I* should be the dragon.

JANE: Don't get excited. We'll figure this out.

WILLIAM: How?

JANE: Maybe we should ask Mr. Parks for help.

SARAH: Mr. Parks is busy with another group. Besides, he told us to work this out among ourselves. We haven't given it much of a chance.

ARTHUR: Well, we can't *all* be the dragon!

SARAH: Why not? Let's rehearse the play with everyone reading the part of the dragon. Then nobody will have anything to complain about.

RHODA: How can we all read the same part? What kind of a play will that be?

SARAH: Let's just try it and see what happens. Everybody look at page one. Ready? Begin!

[long pause]

ARTHUR: Excuse me, Sarah, but I think we've got a problem. Someone has to read the narrator's part, or we can't even get started.

JANE: Well, I've never been a narrator before, so I'll do it. The rest of you can be the dragon. We'll be fine until we get to page 2.

WILLIAM: What happens on page 2?

JANE: Look at the dragon's speech in the middle of the page and you'll find out! Go ahead. You read and I'll listen.

ALL (except Jane): Knock! Knock! Knock!
Is anybody home?

[long pause]

ARTHUR: Oh, I get it! The next line belongs to the witch. If someone doesn't read her part, we won't have a play.

JANE: You got it!

SARAH: What do you think we should do?

RHODA: Wait a minute! William, tell us again why you wanted to be the dragon.

WILLIAM: I like sounding scary.

RHODA: Well, in this play, the scary character is the witch, not the dragon.

WILLIAM: You're right! I was born to play the witch! The rest of you can be the dragon.

JOSH: Now we're getting somewhere.

SARAH: I just read the script again. I think I'd rather have a part all to myself. The bird has some good lines, so I'll be the bird. The rest of you can be the dragon.

ARTHUR: If Jane and William and Sarah all get their own parts, I want a part of my own, too. I'll be the farmer.

JOSH: That means there are only two of us left to read the part of the dragon.

WILLIAM: Don't forget, we still don't have a blacksmith.

JOSH: A blacksmith has to be strong, and we all know I'm the strongest person in this group!

RHODA: Get real!

WILLIAM: Give me a break!   *[together]*

ARTHUR: Sure thing.

SARAH: Come on, Josh.

JOSH: Good, I'm glad you agree. I'll be the blacksmith.

RHODA: And I'll be the dragon!

SARAH: Great. Now, since everybody has a part, let's get to work.

ACT II

NARRATOR: Once upon a time, long, long ago, there lived a handsome dragon with shiny green scales. You would think that such a magnificent dragon would be happy. But this was not so, for a witch had put a spell on the dragon. And a terrible spell it was, too!

DRAGON: Oh, me! Oh, my! Ever since the witch put this spell on me, I can't breathe fire. It really was an accident that my fiery breath burned her brand new broom. Whoever heard of a dragon who can't breathe fire? What am I going to do?

NARRATOR: The dragon spent a great deal of time feeling sorry for himself. Then one day, he had an idea.

DRAGON: Since the witch put this spell on me, she must be able to take it off again! I'll ask her what I can do to get my fire back.

NARRATOR: And so the dragon stomped off through the forest until he came to the witch's cottage.

DRAGON: Knock! Knock! Knock!
Is anybody home?

WITCH: You don't have to knock the door down! Oh, it's you, Dragon. What do you want? After I took your fire away, you said you never wanted to see me again.

DRAGON: It's true. I did say that. But now I've come to do you a favor.

WITCH: You have come to do ME a favor! Ha ha ha! What favor could a dragon who likes to burn brooms do for a witch?

DRAGON: Well, even though I don't have my fire, I am still big and strong. Give me a difficult task. If I can do it, you can give me back my fire.

Macmillan/McGraw-Hill

WITCH: And if you can't?

DRAGON: Then I promise never to bother you again.

WITCH: Very well. It sounds like I can't lose! Let me think. Hmmmmm. . . . There is one little thing that I would like to have.

DRAGON: Name it!

WITCH: There was a little songbird that used to sing outside my window every morning and every evening. But she has flown away. If you can find that songbird and bring her back to me, then I'll lift the spell.

DRAGON: I'm on my way!

NARRATOR: The dragon set off immediately in search of the songbird. After a time, he came to a tall tree beside a river. High up in the tree sat a bird that was singing a beautiful song.

DRAGON: Hello, little songbird.

BIRD: A dragon!

DRAGON: Don't let me scare you. I'm really quite harmless. Tell me, have you lived here all your life?

BIRD: No, Dragon. I used to live in a tree by the witch's cottage.

DRAGON: Why did you leave?

BIRD: I needed some straw to build my nest. But when the witch's broom got burned, she had no straw to give me. So I left in search of some.

DRAGON: The witch misses your singing very much. If I find you some straw, will you go back and build your nest by the witch's cottage? If you do, the witch will give me back my fire.

BIRD: Very well, if you find me some straw, I will build my nest by the witch's cottage, so the witch will give you back your fire.

NARRATOR: The dragon went off in search of some straw. At last he came to a farmer in a field.

DRAGON: Good day to you, Farmer.

FARMER: A dragon!

DRAGON: Don't let me scare you. I'm really quite harmless. And I've only come to ask you a very small favor.

FARMER: What is this small favor?

DRAGON: Will you please cut me some straw,
so the songbird can build her nest,
so the witch will give me back my fire?

FARMER: Very well, but my horse needs new shoes
before he can pull the mower.
If you will shoe my horse,
then I can cut the straw,
so the songbird can build her nest,
so the witch will give you back your fire.

NARRATOR: The dragon took the farmer's horse and
went to find the blacksmith.

DRAGON: Good day to you, Blacksmith.

BLACKSMITH: A dragon!

DRAGON: Don't let me scare you. I'm really quite
harmless. And I've only come to ask you a very
small favor.

BLACKSMITH: What is this small favor?

DRAGON:
Will you please shoe the farmer's horse,
so the farmer can cut his straw,
so the songbird can build her nest,
so the witch will give me back my fire?

Macmillan/McGraw-Hill

BLACKSMITH: I would like to help you, Dragon. But as you can plainly see, my fire has gone out. Until the coals are hot again, I cannot shoe this or any other horse.

DRAGON: If I can get your fire started, will you help me?

BLACKSMITH: Very well, if you can start my fire,
I will shoe the farmer's horse,
so the farmer can cut his straw,
so the songbird can build her nest,
so the witch will give you back your fire.

DRAGON: I'll be back just as soon as I can.

NARRATOR: And with that, the dragon stomped off through the forest. Soon he was standing at the witch's door.

DRAGON: KNOCK! KNOCK! KNOCK!
It's me again.

WITCH: Of course it's you. Nobody else knocks the door DOWN. Well, do you have my songbird?

DRAGON: Almost.

WITCH: ALMOST? Either you have the bird or you don't. And if you don't have the bird, you won't get your fire back.

DRAGON: Dear Witch, I know where your songbird is, and I know how to bring her back.

WITCH: Then what's the problem? Just bring her to me, and I'll return your fire.

DRAGON: It's not as simple as that. You see, to bring her back to you, I must first have my fire.

WITCH: What? Give you back your fire? Why, if I do that, you'll just disappear. Perhaps I should save us both a lot of trouble and make you disappear right now!

DRAGON: Now don't be hasty, or we'll both be unhappy. You'll be unhappy because you won't have your songbird, and I'll be unhappy because I won't have . . . well, I won't have ME!

WITCH: Very well, I guess I'll just have to trust you. Now, open wide, stick out your tongue, and say A-h-h-h-h-h!

DRAGON: Will this hurt?

WITCH: It will sting just a little. After all, you do want to breathe fire, don't you? Now hold still while I wave my magic wand. Fee, fie, foe, FIRE! There! The spell is broken!

DRAGON: WHOOOOOOSH!
Ah, that's more like it. I'm a genuine dragon again. How can I ever thank you?

WITCH: You can start by bringing me my songbird.

DRAGON: Oh yes! In my excitement, I nearly forgot.

NARRATOR: The dragon stomped happily all the way to the blacksmith's shop, breathing fire in a friendly fashion at everyone he met.

BLACKSMITH: Well, I see you've come back. Do you have the fire?

DRAGON: I certainly do! Please stand back!

NARRATOR: And the dragon breathed out a bright, hot flame. Soon the blacksmith's fire was roaring again . . .

BLACKSMITH: so I can shoe the farmer's horse,

FARMER: so I can cut my straw for the bird,

BIRD: so I can build my nest in the tree
by the witch's cottage,

WITCH: so I can listen to my lovely songbird,

DRAGON: so we (especially me) can all live . . .

ALL: happily ever after!

Blocking Diagram

Arrange six chairs or stools, as shown.

1. JANE (Narrator)   4. RHODA (Dragon)
2. SARAH (Bird)   5. ARTHUR (Farmer)
3. WILLIAM (Witch)   6. JOSH (Blacksmith)

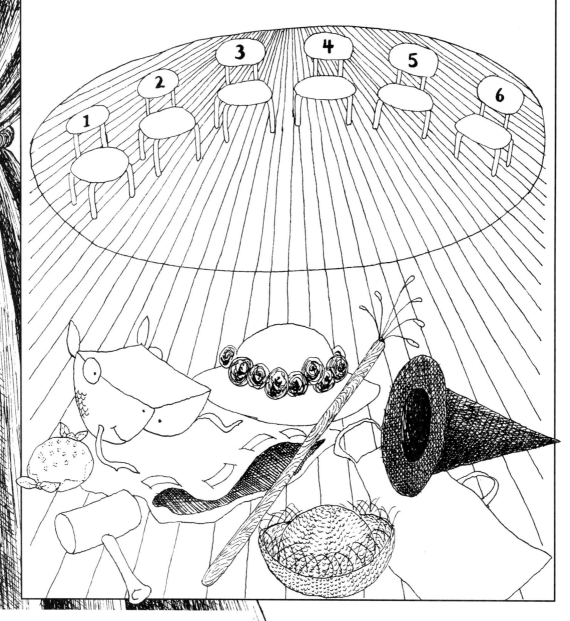

Performance and Costume Suggestions

I'll Be the Dragon! is a two-act play-within-a-play that deals in a humorous way with some of the casting problems that can occur when several children in a Readers Theater group decide that they all want to play the same part! The play can be performed without costumes, but the use of some simple costumes and props can help the audience visualize the transformation of the readers from students rehearsing a play to the cast staging a polished performance.

COSTUME SUGGESTIONS FOR ACT I

All of the readers should be dressed in comfortable school clothes.

COSTUME SUGGESTIONS FOR ACT II

JANE (Narrator)

The narrator does not need a costume, but often a hat from the classroom costume box or from home can help the child feel more in character.

ARTHUR (Farmer)

The child playing the part of the farmer can wear overalls or jeans, a colorful bandana tied around the neck, and a straw hat pushed well back from the face.

WILLIAM (Witch)

Fold a sheet of 12-by-24-inch black construction paper in half. Cut out a quarter circle. Then unfold the paper into a half circle. Roll it to make a cone that will fit the child's head. Tape the cone securely. To make the brim, place the cone on a sheet of stiff black paper and trace around the base of the cone. Draw a larger circle around the first circle you have traced to make the brim. Draw six or seven tabs on the inner circle. Then cut the brim out, making sure the tabs stay in place. Fold the tabs up and slip the brim over the cone. Tape the tabs to the inside of the cone to hold the brim in place.

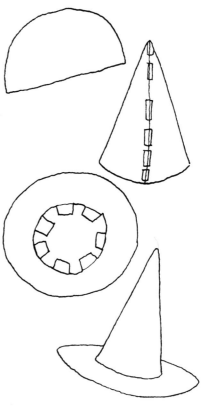

JOSH (Blacksmith)

The blacksmith can wear a sleeveless T-shirt and a bib-top apron. Knot each corner of a handkerchief and use it for the blacksmith's hat.

RHODA (Dragon)

There are many simple costume options for the child playing the part of the dragon. One of the easiest is to make a simple sack for the body with an attached tail.

To make the sack, cut a piece of green fabric as wide as the distance from elbow to elbow as shown. Cut the piece twice as long as the distance from the child's neck to knees.

Fold the fabric in half and stitch the sides together, leaving an opening in each seam for the child's arms. Now cut two holes in the fold along the bottom edge for the child's legs to go through.

Cut slits every three inches near the top edge of the sack and pass a ribbon or length of bias tape through the slits.

Have the child step into the sack. Then stuff it with crumpled tissue paper or newspaper. Draw the ribbon to gather the sack at the top and tie it in a bow. Attach a dragon tail cut from oak tag that has been painted green.

To make the dragon head, cut off one of the side panels from a grocery bag. Then trim the large panels as shown. Cover the bag with green construction paper or paint it green. Use a darker color to outline dragon scales. Glue Ping-Pong balls near the top of the bag for eyes. Then add a pair of dragon-like ears cut from oak tag painted green. Make a small hole on either side of the head and attach ribbons to tie under the child's chin.

SARAH (Bird)

The bird can wear a basic sack body similar to that worn by the dragon. Blue or yellow fabric can be used.

To make the bird hat, cut a headband approximately two inches wide, and long enough to fasten securely around the child's head. Then accordion-fold two 9-by-12-inch sheets of construction paper to make feathers. Attach these feathers to either side of the headband.

THE SEARCH FOR THE MAGIC LAKE

BY MERRILY P. HANSEN
BASED ON AN ECUADORIAN FOLK TALE

EMPEROR

VOICE OF THE FIRE

EMPRESS

SUMAC

MAGICIAN

PRINCE

FIRST SON

SECOND SON

FARMER'S WIFE

FARMER

FIRST SPARROW

SECOND SPARROW

CRAB

SERPENT

ALLIGATOR

GUARD

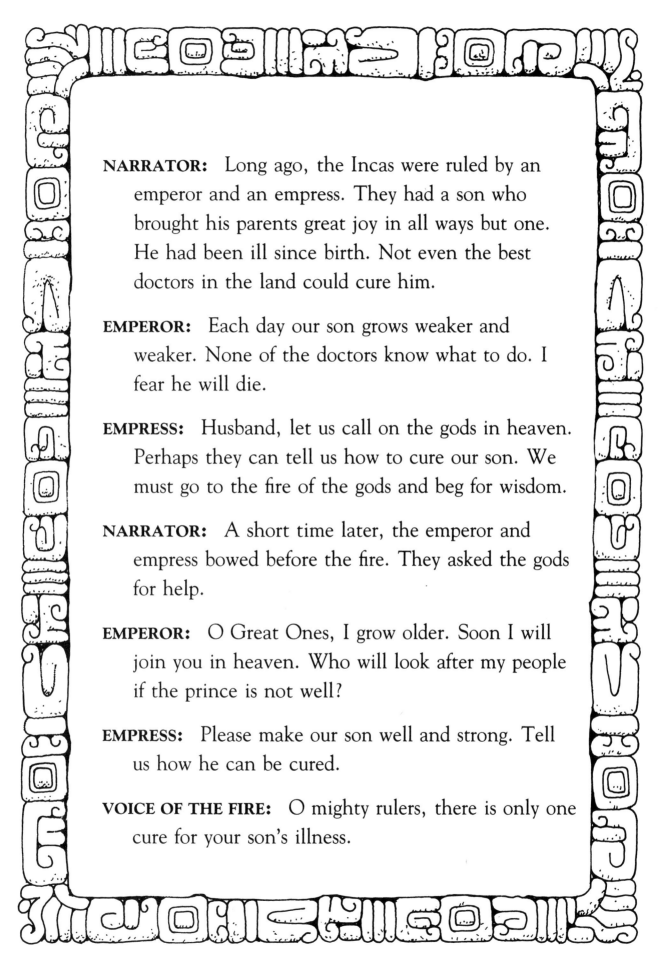

NARRATOR: Long ago, the Incas were ruled by an emperor and an empress. They had a son who brought his parents great joy in all ways but one. He had been ill since birth. Not even the best doctors in the land could cure him.

EMPEROR: Each day our son grows weaker and weaker. None of the doctors know what to do. I fear he will die.

EMPRESS: Husband, let us call on the gods in heaven. Perhaps they can tell us how to cure our son. We must go to the fire of the gods and beg for wisdom.

NARRATOR: A short time later, the emperor and empress bowed before the fire. They asked the gods for help.

EMPEROR: O Great Ones, I grow older. Soon I will join you in heaven. Who will look after my people if the prince is not well?

EMPRESS: Please make our son well and strong. Tell us how he can be cured.

VOICE OF THE FIRE: O mighty rulers, there is only one cure for your son's illness.

EMPEROR: Tell us! We will do anything.

VOICE OF THE FIRE: The prince must drink water from the magic lake at the end of the world. Then he will be cured.

NARRATOR: The fire died and grew cold. But among the ashes lay a golden flask.

EMPRESS: The magic lake at the end of the world? I have never heard of such a place.

EMPEROR: The Voice of the Fire always speaks the truth. We must find the lake so that our son may be cured.

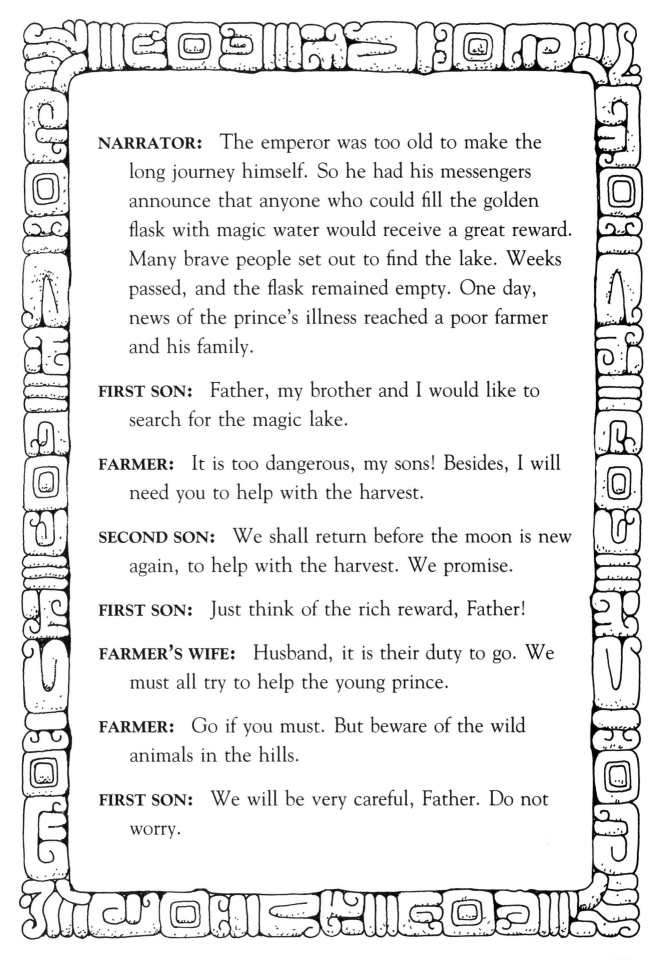

NARRATOR: The emperor was too old to make the long journey himself. So he had his messengers announce that anyone who could fill the golden flask with magic water would receive a great reward. Many brave people set out to find the lake. Weeks passed, and the flask remained empty. One day, news of the prince's illness reached a poor farmer and his family.

FIRST SON: Father, my brother and I would like to search for the magic lake.

FARMER: It is too dangerous, my sons! Besides, I will need you to help with the harvest.

SECOND SON: We shall return before the moon is new again, to help with the harvest. We promise.

FIRST SON: Just think of the rich reward, Father!

FARMER'S WIFE: Husband, it is their duty to go. We must all try to help the young prince.

FARMER: Go if you must. But beware of the wild animals in the hills.

FIRST SON: We will be very careful, Father. Do not worry.

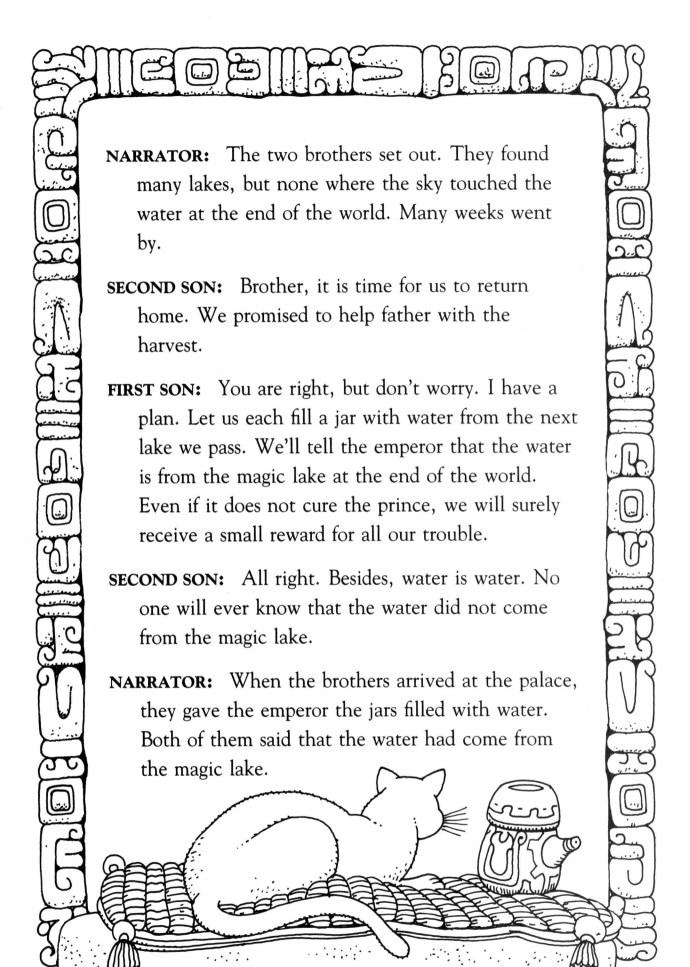

NARRATOR: The two brothers set out. They found many lakes, but none where the sky touched the water at the end of the world. Many weeks went by.

SECOND SON: Brother, it is time for us to return home. We promised to help father with the harvest.

FIRST SON: You are right, but don't worry. I have a plan. Let us each fill a jar with water from the next lake we pass. We'll tell the emperor that the water is from the magic lake at the end of the world. Even if it does not cure the prince, we will surely receive a small reward for all our trouble.

SECOND SON: All right. Besides, water is water. No one will ever know that the water did not come from the magic lake.

NARRATOR: When the brothers arrived at the palace, they gave the emperor the jars filled with water. Both of them said that the water had come from the magic lake.

EMPEROR: Then one sip of water should cure the prince.

EMPRESS: Hurry! Let us give him a taste of it.

NARRATOR: The prince took a sip from each jar of water.

PRINCE: Father, I don't feel any better.

EMPEROR: I have my doubts about this water!

FIRST SON: Your majesty, perhaps the prince should drink it from the golden flask.

SECOND SON: That will probably make all the difference in the world!

NARRATOR: The emperor carefully poured a little water from each jar into the golden flask.

EMPEROR: My goodness! Look what is happening!

EMPRESS: Why, the water is disappearing as you pour it! The flask is still empty.

FIRST SON: That flask must be magic!

SECOND SON: Perhaps your magician could break the spell.

NARRATOR: The emperor called his magician to his side. He told him all that had happened.

MAGICIAN: Your majesty, I cannot break the spell of the golden flask.

EMPEROR: But you are my best magician! Of course you can break the spell.

MAGICIAN: No, your majesty, I cannot. I believe that the flask is telling us that we have been tricked. This is ordinary water! The golden flask can only be filled with water from the magic lake at the end of the world.

EMPEROR: So, you two have dared lie to me! You will spend the rest of your lives in chains. Each day you will drink water from your jars to remind you of your trickery.

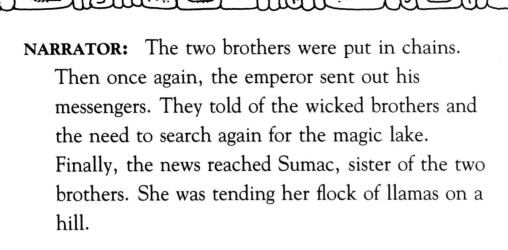

NARRATOR: The two brothers were put in chains. Then once again, the emperor sent out his messengers. They told of the wicked brothers and the need to search again for the magic lake. Finally, the news reached Sumac, sister of the two brothers. She was tending her flock of llamas on a hill.

SUMAC: I must tell Mother and Father the sad news about my brothers. Perhaps they will let me go in search of the magic lake.

NARRATOR: Sumac told her parents all she had heard.

Macmillan/McGraw-Hill

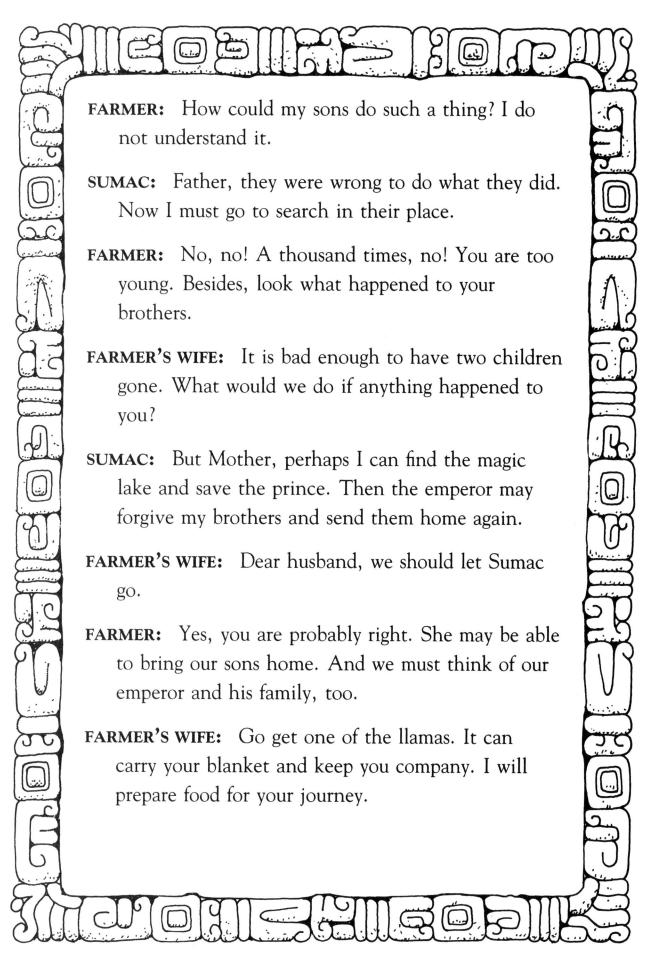

FARMER: How could my sons do such a thing? I do not understand it.

SUMAC: Father, they were wrong to do what they did. Now I must go to search in their place.

FARMER: No, no! A thousand times, no! You are too young. Besides, look what happened to your brothers.

FARMER'S WIFE: It is bad enough to have two children gone. What would we do if anything happened to you?

SUMAC: But Mother, perhaps I can find the magic lake and save the prince. Then the emperor may forgive my brothers and send them home again.

FARMER'S WIFE: Dear husband, we should let Sumac go.

FARMER: Yes, you are probably right. She may be able to bring our sons home. And we must think of our emperor and his family, too.

FARMER'S WIFE: Go get one of the llamas. It can carry your blanket and keep you company. I will prepare food for your journey.

NARRATOR: When the llama was loaded, the family said goodbye. Sumac set out, leading the llama along the trail. The first night, she heard the cry of the wild puma. She feared for her llama, so the next morning she sent it home. The second night, Sumac slept in a tall tree. At sunrise she was awakened by the voices of some sparrows.

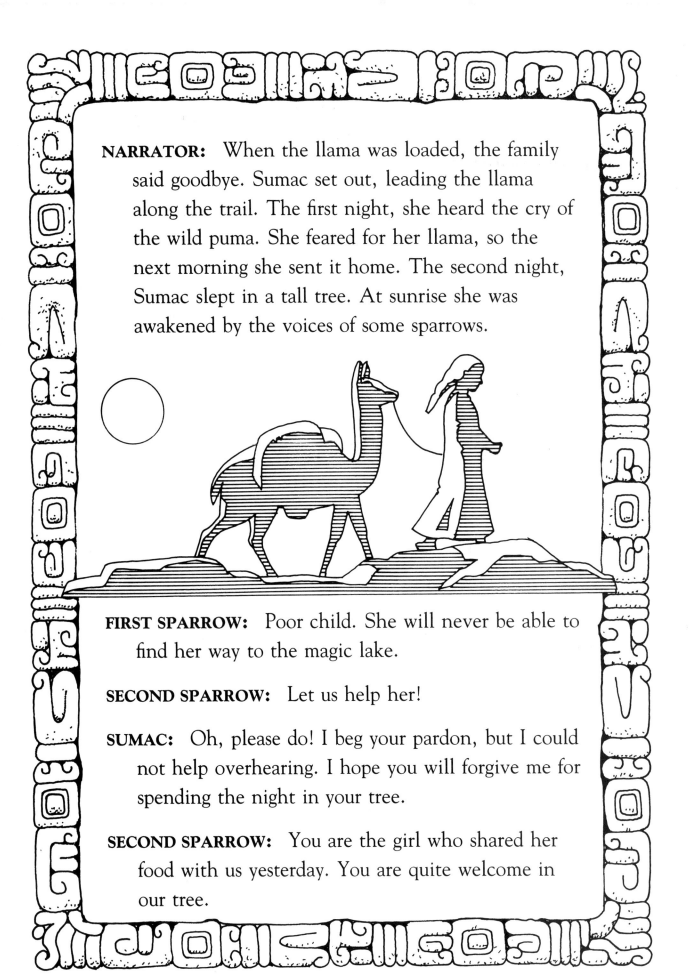

FIRST SPARROW: Poor child. She will never be able to find her way to the magic lake.

SECOND SPARROW: Let us help her!

SUMAC: Oh, please do! I beg your pardon, but I could not help overhearing. I hope you will forgive me for spending the night in your tree.

SECOND SPARROW: You are the girl who shared her food with us yesterday. You are quite welcome in our tree.

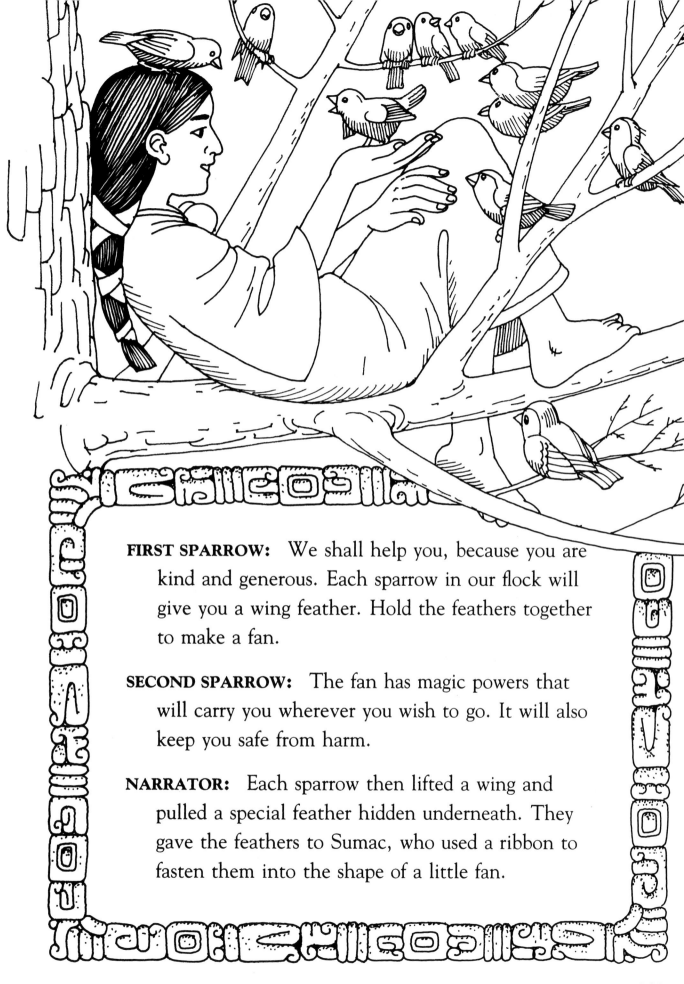

FIRST SPARROW: We shall help you, because you are kind and generous. Each sparrow in our flock will give you a wing feather. Hold the feathers together to make a fan.

SECOND SPARROW: The fan has magic powers that will carry you wherever you wish to go. It will also keep you safe from harm.

NARRATOR: Each sparrow then lifted a wing and pulled a special feather hidden underneath. They gave the feathers to Sumac, who used a ribbon to fasten them into the shape of a little fan.

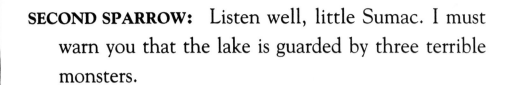

SECOND SPARROW: Listen well, little Sumac. I must warn you that the lake is guarded by three terrible monsters.

FIRST SPARROW: But have no fear. If you hold the magic fan up to your face, you will be safe.

NARRATOR: Sumac thanked the birds for their kindness. Then she spread the fan and held it up.

SUMAC: Please, magic fan. Take me to the lake at the end of the world.

NARRATOR: With that, a soft breeze began to blow. It picked up Sumac and carried her higher and higher into the sky. She looked down and saw the great mountains covered with snow. At last the wind put her down on the shores of a beautiful lake. Sumac looked across the lake to where the sky touched the water.

SUMAC: This must be the lake at the end of the world!

NARRATOR: Sumac carefully tucked the magic fan into her belt. As she did so, she realized that she had forgotten something.

SUMAC: Oh no! I left the jar back in the forest. How will I carry the water back to the prince?

NARRATOR: There was a soft thud at her feet. She looked down and discovered a beautiful golden flask. It was the same one that the emperor had found in the ashes of the fire of the gods. Sumac picked up the flask and went down to the lake. As she bent over, she heard a terrible hissing sound.

CRAB: Just a moment. What do you think you are doing?

NARRATOR: Sumac turned and saw a giant crab. It was as large as a pig and as dark as the night.

CRAB: Get away from my lake, or I shall wrap my long, hairy arms around you and carry you to the bottom!

SUMAC: The sparrows said that the magic fan would protect me. I must trust in their promise.

NARRATOR: Sumac spread the magic fan in front of her face. At once, the crab's eyes began to close.

CRAB: What is happening? I feel so tired . . . I cannot keep my eyes open. Z-Z-Z-Z-Z-Z

NARRATOR: With that, the monster fell to the sand in a deep sleep. Quickly, Sumac began to fill the flask. This time she heard a strange bubbling noise. It was coming from a huge green log floating near the shore. Then the log began to speak.

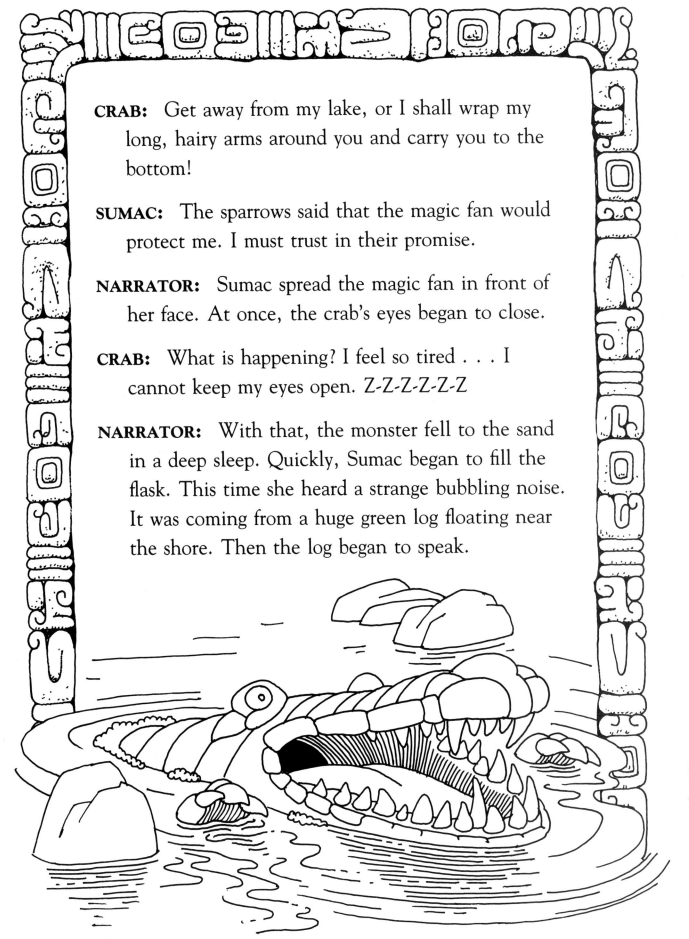

Macmillan/McGraw-Hill

ALLIGATOR: Stop! You may not take water from this lake.

SUMAC: It's another monster! That log is really a giant alligator!

ALLIGATOR: Get away from my lake, or I shall eat you!

SUMAC: I must trust the fan once more.

NARRATOR: Sumac waited until the alligator swam closer. Then she opened the fan and held it up.

ALLIGATOR: What is happening? I feel so tired . . . I cannot keep my eyes open. Z-Z-Z-Z-Z-Z

NARRATOR: With that, the alligator slowly sank to the bottom of the lake in a sound sleep. A third time, Sumac began to fill the flask. All at once, she heard a shrill whistle.

SERPENT: What are you doing? Who gave you leave to take water from the magic lake?

NARRATOR: Sumac looked up. There was a flying serpent. Its scales were as red as fire. Shining sparks flew from its eyes.

SERPENT: Get away from my lake, or I shall bite you!

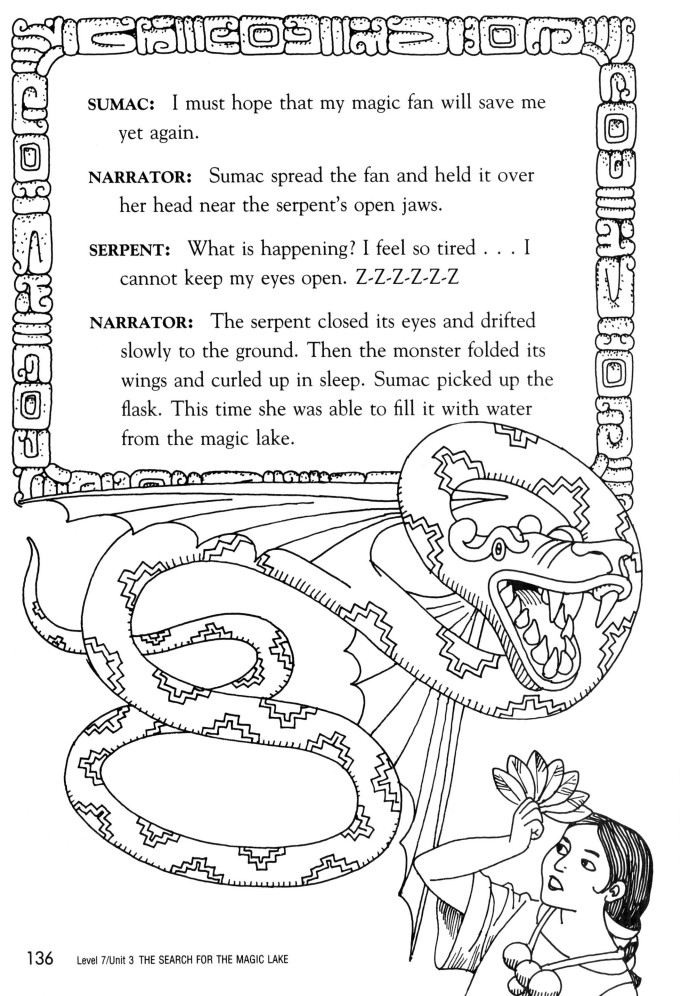

SUMAC: I must hope that my magic fan will save me yet again.

NARRATOR: Sumac spread the fan and held it over her head near the serpent's open jaws.

SERPENT: What is happening? I feel so tired . . . I cannot keep my eyes open. Z-Z-Z-Z-Z-Z

NARRATOR: The serpent closed its eyes and drifted slowly to the ground. Then the monster folded its wings and curled up in sleep. Sumac picked up the flask. This time she was able to fill it with water from the magic lake.

SUMAC: Magic fan, please take me to the palace.

NARRATOR: As Sumac spoke these words, she found herself standing beside the palace gates looking up at a tall guard.

SUMAC: Please, sir, I wish to see the emperor.

GUARD: What business do you have with the emperor, little girl?

SUMAC: I am Sumac. I bring water from the magic lake to cure the prince.

GUARD: Come this way. I'll take you to see the emperor immediately!

NARRATOR: Sumac followed the guard through the palace. Finally, they came to a room with a huge bed. There lay the prince. The emperor and the empress stood by his side.

GUARD: Your majesty, this is Sumac. She brings water from the magic lake!

NARRATOR: Sumac rushed to the bed to give the prince a few drops of the water.

SUMAC: Dear prince! Taste this water. It is from the magic lake at the end of the world.

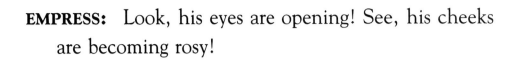

EMPRESS: Look, his eyes are opening! See, his cheeks are becoming rosy!

PRINCE: How strong I feel! This must indeed be water from the magic lake.

EMPEROR: Dear child, you have saved my son's life! All the riches of my kingdom are not enough to reward you. Ask whatever you wish.

SUMAC: Kind emperor, I have but three wishes.

EMPEROR: Name them, and they will be granted.

SUMAC: First, I wish my brothers to be free. They have learned a hard lesson and will never lie again.

EMPEROR: Guards, free the two brothers at once! What is your second wish, my dear?

SUMAC: I wish to have the magic fan returned to the sparrows in the forest.

NARRATOR: Before the emperor could speak, the magic fan floated out through the window, over the trees, and back to the forest.

EMPRESS: What is your last wish, dear Sumac?

SUMAC: I wish my parents to have a large farm with great flocks of llamas, so they will never be poor again.

EMPEROR: It will be so. But I am sure your parents never felt poor with such a wonderful daughter as you.

PRINCE: Sumac, won't you stay with us in the palace?

EMPRESS: Yes, stay with us. We shall do all that we can to make you happy.

SUMAC: Thank you for your kindness. But I must return to my family. I miss them, as I know they have missed me.

NARRATOR: When Sumac returned home, her family was waiting. Her parents now owned a rich farm. A beautiful new house and barn were soon built. And at the palace, the golden flask was never empty. The royal family lived long and happy lives.

BLOCKING DIAGRAM

Arrange the cast on chairs and standing, as shown.

1. VOICE OF THE FIRE
2. MAGICIAN
3. GUARD
4. EMPEROR
5. EMPRESS
6. PRINCE
7. NARRATOR
8. SUMAC
9. FARMER
10. FARMER'S WIFE
11. FIRST SON
12. SECOND SON
13. CRAB
14. CROCODILE
15. SERPENT
16. FIRST SPARROW
17. SECOND SPARROW

PUPPET STAGE DIRECTIONS

It's easy to make a puppet stage from a large cardboard box, such as a refrigerator carton. Cut the carton in half lengthwise to allow ample space for several puppeteers at one time.

Cut a stage opening closer to the top of the panel than the bottom, so that the children have room to move their arms. Set the box on the edge of a table and secure it with tape. The puppeteers will perform from behind the table as the actors read the play.

The children can create two backdrops—one of mountains and the other of a palace interior. Tape the backdrops behind the puppet stage. Stagehands can change the backdrops as needed.

Other spaces can also be turned into puppet theaters. A table becomes a puppet theater when turned on its side and draped with a cloth, sheet, or blanket. An open doorway becomes a stage simply by tacking a cloth or a sheet across it.

To assemble the stick puppets on the following pages, have the children color them, cut them out on the dotted lines, and mount them on oak tag. Then tape each puppet to an unsharpened pencil, a ruler, or a chopstick.

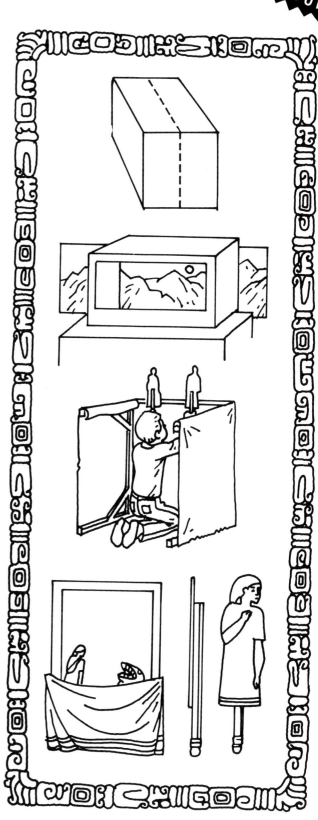

STICK PUPPETS

Directions: Have children cut out each puppet and attach it to a stick.

Macmillan/McGraw-Hill

Directions: Have children cut out each puppet and attach it to a stick.

Directions: Have children cut out each puppet and attach it to a stick.

Directions: Have children cut out each puppet and attach it to a stick.

Directions: Have children cut out each puppet and attach it to a stick.

Directions: Have children cut out each puppet and attach
it to a stick.

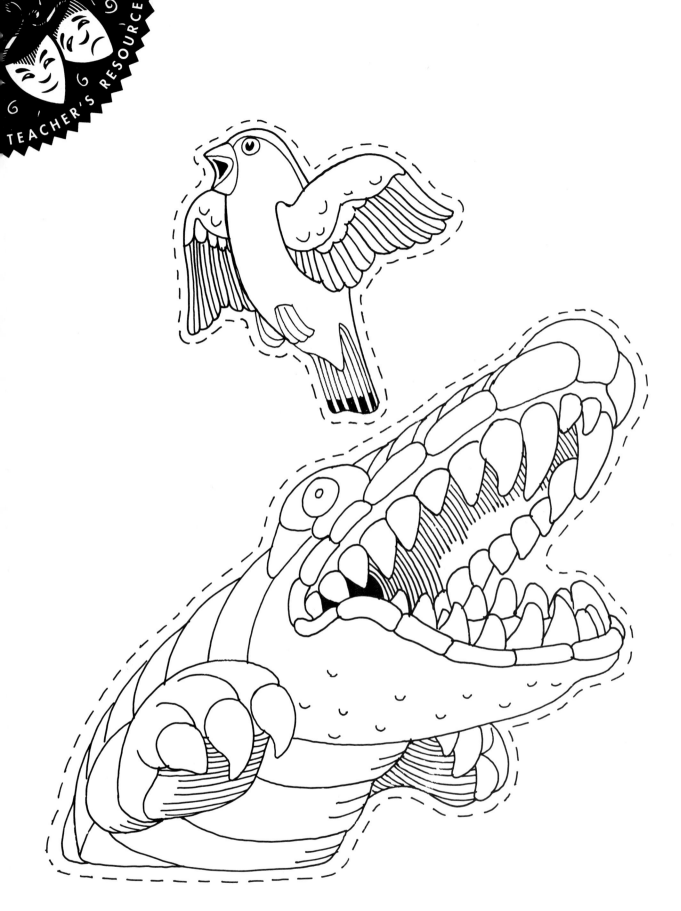

Directions: Have children cut out each puppet and attach it to a stick.

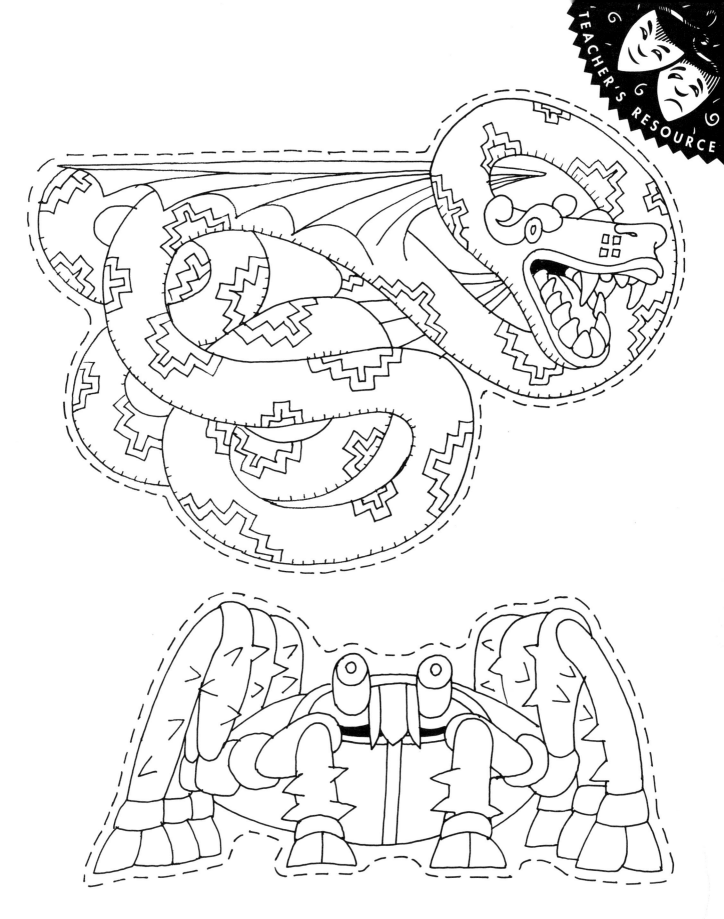

Directions: Have children cut out each puppet and attach it to a stick.

CHORAL READING
BLOCKING DIAGRAMS

LEVEL 6 / UNIT 1
Hush Little Baby

group 1 | group 2

LEVEL 6 / UNIT 2
The Secret Song

group 1 | group 2

LEVEL 6 / UNIT 3
ᵀHₑ **ERIE CANAL**

group 1 | group 2 | group 3

LEVEL 6 / UNIT 2
KNOWING

group 1 | group 2 | group 3

LEVEL 7 / UNIT 1

My Autograph Album

| group 1 | group 2 |

LEVEL 7 / UNIT 2

HELPING

| group 1 | group 2 | group 3 | group 4 |

LEVEL 7 / UNIT 3

One Misty, Moisty Morning

| group 1 | group 2 | group 3 |

LEVEL 7 / UNIT 2

CHANGING

| group 1 | group 2 |

LEVEL 7 / UNIT 3

Sound of Water

| group 1 | group 2 | group 3 | group 4 |

Hush Little Baby

Group 1: Hush little baby, don't say a word,
Mama's gonna buy you a mockingbird.

Group 2: And if that mockingbird won't sing,
Mama's gonna buy you a diamond ring.

Group 1: And if that diamond ring turns brass,
Mama's gonna buy you a looking glass.

Group 2: And if that looking glass gets broke,
Mama's gonna buy you a billy goat.

Group 1: And if that billy goat won't pull,
Mama's gonna buy you a cart and bull.

Group 2: And if that cart and bull turn over,
Mama's gonna buy you a dog named Rover.

Group 1: And if that dog named Rover won't bark,
Mama's gonna buy you a horse and cart.

Group 2: And if that horse and cart fall down,
You'll still be the sweetest little baby in town.

Traditional

The Secret Song

Group 1: Who saw the petals
               drop from the rose?

Group 2: I, said the spider,
               But nobody knows.

Group 1: Who saw the sunset
               flash on the bird?

Group 2: I, said the fish,
               But nobody heard.

Group 1: Who saw the fog
               come over the sea?

Group 2: I, said the pigeon,
               Only me.

Group 1: Who saw the first
               green light of the sun?

Group 2: I, said the night owl,
               The only one.

Group 1: Who saw the moss
               creep over the stone?

Group 2: I, said the grey fox,
               All alone.

Margaret Wise Brown

KNOWING

Group 1: Nobody teaches
a bird to sing
or a frog to croak
as soon as it's spring.

Group 2: Nobody teaches
a bee to make honey
or shows how-to-hop
to a new little bunny.

Group 3: Nobody teaches
a spider to spin . . .

All: How do they know
what to do to *begin?*

Aileen Fisher

T_H_E ERIE CANAL

Group 1: I've got a mule, her name is Sal,

All: Fifteen years on the Erie Canal.

Group 1: She's a good old worker and a good old pal,

All: Fifteen years on the Erie Canal.

Group 1: We've hauled some barges in our day,
Filled with lumber, coal, and hay,
And every inch of the way I know
From Albany to Buffalo.

All: Low bridge, everybody down!
Low bridge, for we're comin' to a town!
You can always tell your neighbor, can
        always tell your pal,
If you've ever navigated on the Erie Canal.

Macmillan/McGraw-Hill

Group 2: We'd better look for a job, old gal,

    All: Fifteen years on the Erie Canal.

Group 2: You bet your life I wouldn't part with Sal,

    All: Fifteen years on the Erie Canal.

Group 2: Giddap there, Sal, we've passed that lock,

           We'll make Rome 'fore six o'clock,

           So one more trip and then we'll go

           Right straight back to Buffalo.

    All: Low bridge, everybody down!

           Low bridge, for we're comin' to a town!

           You can always tell your neighbor, can

              always tell your pal,

           If you've ever navigated on the Erie Canal.

Group 3: Where would I be if I lost my pal?

    All: Fifteen years on the Erie Canal.

Group 3: Oh, I'd like to see a mule as good as Sal,

    All: Fifteen years on the Erie Canal.

Group 3: A friend of mine once got her sore,

           Now he's got a broken jaw,

           'Cause she let fly with her iron toe

           And kicked him into Buffalo.

    All: Low bridge, everybody down!

           Low bridge, for we're comin' to a town!

           You can always tell your neighbor, can

              always tell your pal,

           If you've ever navigated on the Erie Canal.

Author unknown

My Autograph Album

All: It tickles me,
It makes me laugh,
To think you want
My autograph.

Group 1:   Roses are red,
Violets are blue,
Sugar is sweet,
And so are you.

Group 2:   Roses are red,
Violets are blue,
Grass is green,
And so are you.

Group 1:   I love you little,
I love you big,
I love you like
A little pig.

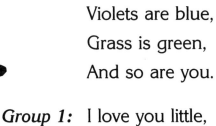

Group 2:   I love you, I love you,
I love you so well;
If I had a peanut,
I'd give you the shell.

Group 1: Just as the mouse
Runs over the rafter,
Group 2: You are the very one
I'm after.

Group 1: Just as the vine
Grows 'round the stump,
Group 2: You are my darling
Sugar lump.

Group 1: You be the ice cream,
Group 2: I'll be the freezer;
Group 1: You be the lemon,
Group 2: And I'll be the squeezer.

Group 1: Some write for pleasure,
Group 2: Some write for fame,
Group 1: But I write only
Group 2: To sign my name.

Group 1: Can't think,
Brain numb;
Group 2: Inspiration
Won't come.
Group 1: Poor ink,
Bad pen;
Group 2: That's all.
All: Amen.

HELPING

Group 1: Agatha Fry, she made a pie,

Group 2: And Christopher John helped bake it.

                Christopher John, he mowed the lawn,

Group 1: And Agatha Fry helped rake it.

Group 3: Zachary Zugg took out the rug,

Group 4: And Jennifer Joy helped shake it.

                And Jennifer Joy, she made a toy,

Group 3: And Zachary Zugg helped break it.

Groups 1 and 2: And some kind of help

                      Is the kind of help

                      That helping's all about.

Groups 3 and 4: And some kind of help

                      Is the kind of help

                      We all can do without.

Shel Silverstein

CHANGING

Group 1: I know what *I* feel like;
I'd like to be *you*
And feel what *you* feel like
And do what *you* do.

Group 2: I'd like to change places
For maybe a week
And look like your look-like
And speak as you speak.

Group 1: And think what you're thinking
And go where you go

Group 2: And feel what you're feeling
And know what you know.

All: I wish we could do it;
What fun it would be

Group 1: If I could try you out

Group 2: And you could try me.

Mary Ann Hoberman

One Misty, Moisty Morning

Group 1: One misty, moisty morning,
When cloudy was the weather,

Group 2: I chanced to meet an old man
Clothed all in leather;

Group 3: Clothed all in leather,
With a strap beneath his chin,

Group 1: How do you do,

Group 2: And how do you do,

Group 3: And how do you do again?

All: How do you do,
And how do you do,
And how do you do again?

Traditional

Sound of Water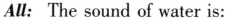

All: The sound of water is:

Group 1: Rain,
Group 2: Lap,
Group 3: Fold,
Group 4: Slap,

Group 1: Gurgle,
Group 2: Splash,
Group 3: Churn,
Group 4: Crash,

Group 1: Murmur,
Group 2: Pour,
Group 3: Ripple,
Group 4: Roar,

Group 1: Plunge,
Group 2: Drip,
Group 3: Spout,
Group 4: Skip,

Group 1: Sprinkle,
Group 2: Flow,
Group 3: Ice,
Group 4: Snow.

Mary O'Neill

Thinking
ABOUT MY OWN PERFORMANCE

Use this sheet to help you think about your performance as:

A Reader	A Listener	A Team Member

My Read-Aloud Skills

	yes	no	sometimes
Did I read smoothly?	yes	no	sometimes
Did I know most words in my part?	yes	no	sometimes
Did I read at the right speed?	yes	no	sometimes
Did I read loudly enough?	yes	no	sometimes
Did I pay attention to punctuation marks?	yes	no	sometimes
Did I sound like my character would sound?	yes	no	sometimes

My Listening Skills

	yes	no	sometimes
Did I listen for my cues?	yes	no	sometimes
Did I listen to myself as I read?	yes	no	sometimes
Did I listen when others read?	yes	no	sometimes

My Teamwork Skills

	yes	no	sometimes
Did I work with others on my team?	yes	no	sometimes
Did I share and take turns?	yes	no	sometimes
Did I do my share of the work?	yes	no	sometimes
Did I try to be helpful?	yes	no	sometimes
Did I listen to what others had to say?	yes	no	sometimes

Think about one way your performance got better. Write about it.

_____

_____

Pick a goal for next time. Write about it.

_____

_____

Macmillan/McGraw-Hill